PRAISE FOR
E-COMMERCE
WEBSITE OPTIMIZATION

"The most comprehensive introduction to e-commerce conversion optimization. Most optimization gurus only talk of A/B testing, but Dan and Johann go far beyond and explain what conversion optimization for e-commerce really means. Highly recommended for anyone trying to get a sense of what they should be doing when optimizing their online store."
Paras Chopra, Founder and CEO, VWO

"If your competitors are running more structured tests than you, you are falling behind. Follow the tried and tested process in *e-Commerce Website Optimization* to get ahead. To maximise your ROI from structured tests, the details matter. I recommend this book as the first practical guide dedicated to CRO for online retail."
Dr Dave Chaffey, CEO, SmartInsights.com

"Having worked closely with the authors it is clear to see that this book lives and breathes what they put in to practice on a daily basis. They and their teams not only understand optimization, but understand our business commercially and apply these techniques to our own business priorities. This book is a must-have for both small and large businesses and has managed to capture both the technical expertise and the methodologies required to run very successful optimization programmes. It is both practical and thorough and can be followed at all levels."
John Donnellan, Director E-Commerce EMEA, Canon Europe

"The authors have done a highly credible job of applying a data-driven digital strategy to e-commerce. From popular topics like A/B testing to obscure tactics like merchandise analysis, the reader is exposed to a veritable plethora of initiatives that will improve business performance.

An aspiring analyst or manager will relish the opportunity to apply the techniques in this book to any e-commerce business."
Kevin Hillstrom, President, MineThatData

"Driving more conversions comes down to an obsession with people, and not visits. Johann and Dan's new book explores this subtle but critical difference in depth. Understand people, their behaviour, their feedback, their testing choices – and win bigger revenues."
Avinash Kaushik, Digital Marketing Evangelist, Google, and author of *Web Analytics 2.0* and *Web Analytics: An Hour a Day*

"I wish I could have read this book before I started my career in e-commerce. Conversion rate optimization is a complicated and complex field and this book is the go-to guide on how to approach it in a palatable way. Finally someone has turned theory into a practical step-by-step guide to improve your business and increase your revenue. Should be prescribed reading for anyone wanting to be top of his game."
Manuel Koser, Co-Founder and MD, Silvertree Internet Holdings

"The whole 9 yards on improving your on line trading performance."
Julian Richer Founder and Managing Director Richer Sounds Plc

"Twenty years of Conversion Rate Optimisation experience is the best you can ask from an expert . . . unless you put Dan Croxen-John and Johann van Tonder together, and then you get forty years. Whether you want to attract the best people to your site, test a variety of user interactions or just want to sell more, this book is the step-by-step guide to increasing revenue, lowering costs and improving customer satisfaction. It's not just a good read, it's a handbook. Keep it on your desk."
Jim Sterne Founder, eMetrics Summit Board Chair, Digital Analytics Association

e-Commerce Website Optimization

e-Commerce Website Optimization

Why 95 per cent of your website
visitors don't buy and what you can do
about it

Dan Croxen-John
and Johann van Tonder

KoganPage

First published in Great Britain and the United States in 2017 by Kogan Page Limited

2nd Floor	c/o Martin P Hill Consulting	4737/23 Ansari Road
45 Gee Street	122 W 27th St., 10th Floor	19102 Daryaganj
London	New York, NY 10001	New Delhi
EC1V 3RS	USA	India
United Kingdom		

ISBN   978 0 7494 7538 3
E-ISBN   978 0 7494 7539 0

British Library Cataloguing-in-Publication Data

A CIP record for this book is available from the British Library.

Library of Congress Control Number

2016958921

Typeset by Integra Software Services Pvt Ltd, India
Print production managed by Jellyfish
Printed and bound in Great Britain by Ashford Colour Press Ltd.

CONTENTS

LIST OF FIGURES

LIST OF TABLES

FOREWORD

Quick, what company is the most successful ecommerce firm on the planet? You probably came up with Amazon, with no hesitation at all.

Next question: when was the last time Amazon redesigned their web site? I'd guess that one made you pause and scratch your head. It seems like they haven't redesigned in a decade or more. Despite their utilitarian and seemingly unchanging website, Amazon has been remarkably successful.

What is their secret?

Of course, Amazon does many things very well. One of the most important, though, is constant testing for the purpose of conversion rate optimization – the art and science of finding the conversion killers on a site, proposing ideas to improve results and then testing those ideas.

And the real answer to the 'time since the last redesign' question is likely 'Yesterday'. Amazon's site seems unchanging simply because it's constantly evolving in small ways. Tests are running all the time at Amazon as well as at many of the other top ecommerce companies.

It's been over a decade since the term 'conversion rate optimization' was coined, and it's gone on to become an integral part of digital marketing.

Now, Dan Croxen-John and Johann van Tonder have created an eminently practical guide to conversion rate optimization for ecommerce websites. They include everything one needs to know, from the software tools to use, the best ways to do research, to how to create high-performing tests. They show you how to optimize the optimization.

As founder and COO of the international agency AWA digital, Dan and Johann have a wealth of expertise to pass on. I first met them when I was invited to speak at one of their regular company get-togethers. Clearly, this is a team that truly understands that 95% of human decision processes are non-conscious and how important it is to build that understanding into your marketing.

Dan and Johann's book is a significant contribution to unravelling the mystery of why so many of your web visitors don't buy and what you can do about it. Getting people to part with their cash is hard, and the most important tool we have is knowledge – knowledge about customers, the way their brains work and how they behave. Now some of that valuable knowledge is available to everyone in this complete, detailed and instructive book.

CRO can deliver long-lasting benefits to any digital business. Because CRO measures actual customer behaviour, it can go beyond merely improving sales. Testing can actually lead to a deeper understanding of customer needs and motivations. This aligns perfectly with the field of neuromarketing, which focuses on going beyond what consumers say they like or want to understand what drives their real-world behavior.

Applying the material in this book in your business will do more than boost short-term results. It has the potential to bring you long-term increases in revenue, competitive advantage and customer loyalty. If you want to both understand the science and take action, you can do no better than read this book.

Roger Dooley, author of *Brainfluence*

INTRODUCTION

We wrote this book for our younger selves. In the past we have both run online businesses where our challenge was to increase sales massively. We were working in two different continents but both of us were under intense pressure to find some way of growing our businesses.

A book like this did not exist at the time and if it had we would have devoured it. If you are the person we were then, we have written this for you. Our vision was to to write a step-by-step guide, with clear guidance on how to get more of your 95 per cent non-buying visitors to convert into customers.

Some warned us that writing a book that gives away our knowledge, reveals our secret sauce and expertise, would hurt our agency by enabling potential clients to do it for themselves. That never worried us.

Every day we see how frustrated people get when using e-commerce websites. Not only in terms of their experience of using the site but also the difficulty, stress even, of making buying decisions. Solving these problems is what drives us. At our agency, we talk about 'buying should be easy' – because we believe it should be. To do that, we have developed an e-commerce website optimization process, refined over many years. This is what we are sharing with you.

Follow our programme and watch your revenue go up. We routinely see our clients achieving double-digit revenue increases within 12 months. Implement the process and see your online sales grow this year, next year and into the future.

Everything you're about to read, we had to learn the hard way. We hope this book can make your own challenge to increase online sales easier than it was for us. If you have any questions, or would like to share how this book has benefited your business, please e-mail either of us – dan.croxenjohn@awa-digital.com or johann.vantonder@awa-digital.com. We would be happy to hear from you and help you in any way we can.

ACKNOWLEDGEMENTS

This book would not have been possible without the work of a small army of talented and committed individuals. We owe a huge debt of gratitude to Mel Henson, our editor. Throughout the process she has encouraged, challenged and supported us. Her tireless enthusiasm has kept us going when the tunnel was not so bright. Our thanks also go to our publishers, Kogan Page. Jenny Volich, Jasmin Naim and Charlotte Owen have provided us with valuable guidance in crafting a set of ideas into what is our first book.

The team at AWA have kept the business going whilst we buried ourselves away in different offices, farmhouses and hotels to concentrate on the writing. Thanks goes to Lynne Wright, Brendan McNulty, John Barnes, Dave Mullen, Hugh Gage, Bill Coloe, Monique Szenkowska, Jim Semlyen, Isobel Wormald and Luke Vaughan.

Our clients have been an inspiration to us – ready to listen to advice and run tests that were daring and bold – thanks for your trust in us. We would especially like to thank Rod Taylor, Clare Dixey, Ben Freeborn, Chris Jarvis and Tracey Robinson.

In writing this book we have stood on the shoulders of giants. We have been fortunate enough to work in an industry dominated by some outstanding thinkers, people who share their immense knowledge widely and without ego. Thanks goes to Bryan and Jeffery Eisenberg, Avinash Kaushik, Peep Laja, Tim Ash, Dr Flint McLauglin, Craig Sullivan, BJ Fogg, Steve Krug, Dr Karl Blanks, Chris Goward, Andrew Wilson, Dr Dave Chaffey, Dan Barker and Kevin Hillstrom. We are also grateful for the support and kind permissions from our friends at Qubit, Optimizely, Maxymiser, Visual Website Optimizer, Qualaroo, Crazy Egg, EyeQuant and Ethnio – the tools you provide us with make what we do possible.

Johann: Thank you Andrea, and my children Brandt, Mickey and Silke for your patience. For two years, I spent many late evenings and weekends away from you to write this book.

Dan: Writing this book took two years of my life and would not have been possible without the support of friends and family. I would like to especially thank my children, Cerys and Huw, for their patience as well as Chris Fordy, Judith Clough, Rupert Bryan, Mark Blowers, Mark Jenner, Nigel Apperley, Tom Lininsh and especially Rachel Trudgill. Thanks also to John Croxen, Mary John, Adam Croxen and Nicola Kent for willing me on.

Introduction to e-commerce website optimization

01

You're reading this because you run, own or have some responsibility for an e-commerce site. You want your website and mobile site to work harder, please more people and generate more cash.

You know that around 95 per cent or more of the visitors who come to your site don't buy. That doesn't change when you throw more money at getting more eyes on the site. Whatever changes you have made to try and improve things have delivered mixed results. You keep bumping your head against these walls:

How can you get more of your visitors to place an order?

How can you get those who bought once to buy again and spend more when they do?

The answer is in this book. It's not a silver bullet. You won't find a list of tactics that will magically make you more money. Alas, there are no latest User Experience (UX) best-practice tips that will do the trick.

What you will get is a step-by-step guide to the structured approach used by companies all over the world. It's a proven and foolproof approach that's not based on the latest fads but on scientific principles that enable you to do what's best for you. Follow it and you, like others before you, will have a guaranteed way to continually improve your online sales.

E-commerce website optimization

You may know about website optimization, or Conversion Rate Optimization (CRO). Perhaps you've dabbled in it. Over the last decade or so, it has gone from being the latest buzzword to becoming integral to the way e-commerce companies do business. Over 90 per cent of marketers now say that CRO is important if not crucial to their organization.[1]

So what exactly is it?

In the e-commerce context, CRO can be defined as a system for influencing (or 'converting') a higher proportion of your visitors to buy more and spend more. It has nothing to do with bringing additional people to the site – it's all about generating more sales from the visitors you already have.

How does it work?

The first step in the process is identifying ideas to improve the site's ability to generate revenue. How you come up with those ideas and how you decide which ones to focus on, is largely what determines success. A big part of this book is therefore devoted to this concept. You then test those ideas on actual visitors in real time to see whether they work. If they do, the tests also give you an indication of just how effective they really are.

In just a few weeks from now, you could have a bank of valuable ideas with definite potential – not hunches or rules about best practice that may or may not be relevant to you. Soon you will start to discover what makes your visitors take out their credit card, as well as some things that make them keep it firmly in their wallet.

Overview of the process

Most CRO systems use the tried and tested 'Scientific Method'. Although different firms give their method different names, the principles are the same. This method has helped scientists in fields as diverse as social sciences, geology and chemistry to come up with new ways of understanding the world and, ultimately, improving aspects of our life.

Central to The Scientific Method is a reliance on measurable evidence, hypotheses and theories,[2] as illustrated below:

Step 1: Define the question

One question drives all CRO efforts in e-commerce: 'How do we make more money?' Everything you do on your optimization programme is aimed at answering this question. Often the unit of measurement for the extra sales generated is Revenue Per Visitor (RPV).

Figure 1.1 The scientific method used in CRO

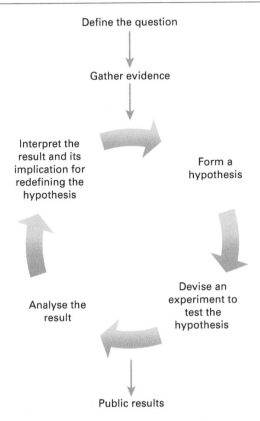

Define the question

Gather evidence

Interpret the
result and its
implication for
redefining the
hypothesis

Form a
hypothesis

Analyse the
result

Devise an
experiment to
test the
hypothesis

Public results

SOURCE Adapted from Lars Christensen, *The Hands-On Guide for Science Communicators*,
Springer, 2007

Step 2: Gather evidence

Data from a variety of sources hold the key to finding out how to improve
your average spend per visitor. Relying on guess work, opinions and even
so-called best practice is like playing the lottery. You may win a bit of money
here and there but it's all down to chance. By following an evidence-led
approach, you remove luck from the scene and bet only on things that you
know are likely to make a big difference.

In the next chapter, we show you the types of tools you can use to get
your hands on the data you need. Chapters 4–6 cover a range of research
methods in detail.

From this, you'll gather a huge amount of data which you need to go through
and tie all the strands together to create a plan or roadmap for the months
ahead. The detailed process of prioritizing what to work on first – and what to
ignore – and then creating an Optimization Plan is covered in Chapter 7.

Step 3: Formulate a hypothesis

Based on what you've observed, you create a hypothesis which predicts the outcome of a proposed change on the website. Make your prediction rationally, as a sensible estimate based on evidence, rather than an optimistic hope, built on your emotional desires. The prediction is tied to an appropriate metric, such as RPV, which is a number you can track in order to measure the effect, if any, of introducing something different. This process is explained in detail in Chapter 8.

Step 4: Experiment

You may be spot on with your hypothesis or totally wide of the mark. No one knows until you put it to the test and run a scientific experiment. The results will either support or refute your hypothesis – but either way, you'll learn something about what makes your customers buy more and spend more on your site.

In the world of CRO, the experiment usually takes the form of an A/B split test. Half your visitors see your current page, and half see the new variation which incorporates changes that you predict will improve RPV. The test group has no idea they are seeing something different, as it appears to them seamlessly integrated into the main website.

Yet behind the scenes, the technology is carefully monitoring who has seen which version, how they are behaving and, crucially, how much they are spending. After a short period of time, you compare results to see how the variation has altered their behaviour and which test group has spent more.

Step 5: Analyse the result

The experiment you run could have one of three outcomes:

- The new variation is a 'winner' and your hypothesis is substantiated.
- The new variation does not 'win' and the hypothesis is refuted.
- There is no difference between the new variation and control; it is inconclusive.

On face value, it looks like you should have your fingers crossed for a win all the time. Yay! Crack open the champagne, make the test page live on your main site and watch all those visitors start spending.

In fact, you should do your best to avoid this kind of 'triumph and disaster' thinking and treat wins and negative uplifts in the same way. Long-term success comes out of being truly scientific. Hoping for a positive result means you've emotionally invested in the result, which introduces a form of bias.

Whatever the outcome, make it your aim to bank the learning and move forward.

A win can often point the way to further tests around the same hypothesis that could give you even bigger uplifts. Tests that don't win are also valuable. There is usually a lot you can learn from them, insight you can use to design another variation that really rakes in the cash.

Step 6: Interpret the result

The purpose of a scientific study is often to contribute new knowledge: CRO is no different. Whether you have substantiated or rejected the hypothesis, with every concluded test you know more about your customers than you did before. Gradually, you will learn vast amounts about what works for your customers and what doesn't.

Step 7: Record the result

In the scientific community, the contribution of new knowledge is formalized by publishing the details of the experiment. Similarly, your work is not complete until you have documented your result. This includes recording the insights from each experiment to share with your colleagues in other parts of the business.

Remember your central question: 'How do we make more money?' With each experiment you collect new knowledge about your customers. Over time, this leads you to make long-term improvements in the site and generate increasing amounts of money from them.

The rest of this book tells you exactly how to implement those seven steps into your own organization, with practical examples, step-by-step instructions and case studies from real e-commerce optimization projects.

Summary

A huge majority of your visitors don't buy what you've got to offer. This book talks you through a proven system to help you to change that for the better and achieve substantially more revenue.

It is based on The Scientific Method, which has been used for years by scientists in many disciplines, to develop new ways of understanding and improving aspects of our lives.

It involves seven steps, anchored by the central question: 'How do we make more money?' You start with research and analysis to gather evidence in order to identify the most valuable ways to improve, or optimize, your site.

This gives you a host of ideas and, to make best use of your time, you rely on a system to prioritize which ones to work on first. In a scientific experiment, ideas are then tested in real time on the visitors to your mobile and web sites.

Some of these ideas will generate higher revenues in the experiment and can go live on your site. Others may not give you the result you expected but will give you unique insights into your customers which could be the start of the next big winner.

Notes

1   E-consultancy (2015), 'Conversion Rate Optimization Report 2015' https://
    econsultancy.com/reports/conversion-rate-optimization-report/ (Accessed: 1 July
    2016).

2   Gauch, Hugh G (2012) Scientific Method in Brief, Cambridge University Press.

The kick-off 02

You're now on the road to optimizing your website, so in a few months' time you should start seeing your sales graph heading skyward and your bonus is looking like a sure-fire thing.

But before you get going you need to get your stall set out. That means defining the project, working out the resources you need and getting some 'tools' on to your website. Tools are pieces of software such as surveys and heatmaps to help you discover what's going on in the minds of your customers.

Get the team in place

CRO is a team effort, so at the beginning of the project, get everyone together for a team kick-off meeting. Your team may be all in-house staff or may include some outside consultants depending on your resources and skills. One individual could take on several roles. Below are the roles that should be represented at this meeting.

Champion

To make sure your CRO succeeds, have some top level support. CRO means change. Don't underestimate how emotionally invested some of your colleagues may be in 'their' website. They can be highly resistant to introducing new elements or new ways of working. Or they may profess to be eager to do things differently but are more interested in their own ideas and hunches rather than what the research tells you. Get support from the C-suite to make sure your programme doesn't get derailed before it's had time to prove itself and delivered the sales growth you're looking for.

Project manager

This person is responsible for keeping the process on track, coordinating team efforts and getting things done on time and on spec. They make sure that the optimization road map is kept up to date.

Researcher

Research is at the heart of The Scientific Method. In CRO, this could include surveys, usability testing, interviews, heatmaps, store visits, customer immersion and competitor research. On a small project, one person, perhaps drawing on ad hoc support from freelancers, might well carry out all the research. On larger projects the work could be shared by several people, overseen by one person who brings it all together.

Data analyst

Research unleashes data. Raw data is useless until it's processed, synthesized and interpreted. Your project will also rely on clickstream data from analytics packages such as Google Analytics that need to be assimilated into the bigger picture. Even small websites generate mountains of quantitative data that will be very useful in the hands of a data analyst.

Developer

Much of the research mentioned above – heatmaps, surveys and so on – as well as split-testing is facilitated by three software tools that you put on your website. Putting these tools on your site is a quick and easy job if you have a basic knowledge of coding – but if you don't know your HTML from your JavaScript then invite your web developer along to the kick-off meeting.

Copywriter

Small copy changes can bring about big results and some of the highest uplifts have been down to words alone. One famous study[1] got a 45 per cent increase in revenue, amounting to over $300m, simply by changing the word on a button from 'Register' to 'Continue' and adding a few lines of text.

In the early stages of the project the copywriter may review all the copy on the website, assessing its strengths and weaknesses against established copywriting principles.

Later on the copywriter's role is chiefly to work with the optimizer to turn placeholder messages indicating a desired action into compelling copy based on sound direct marketing principles. Much of this is microcopy: tiny phrases that guide the customer at key points: with so few words available to achieve so much each one counts.

Designer

If you have in-house designers on your team you may want to invite them along to the kick-off to make sure they are on board with the project.

However, it's worth explaining that their usual boundless creativity is not what will be required on the project. Designers by nature want to come up with new visuals but often that could hinder optimization, not help it.

That's because any new web pages created are born out of detailed research and analysis. They start life as a wireframe, a diagram showing the key elements of a new web page.

When the new page goes into split testing, any visitor who sees it should not be aware that they are a guinea pig. It therefore needs to look as similar to the current one as possible, just with the specific changes needed. Brand guidelines and corporate identity have to be respected down to the last pixel, as well as accurately incorporating all the functionality dictated by the wireframe.

The job of translating a wireframe into a finished new web page is skilled work but it requires attention to detail rather than artistic talent. A creative graphic designer would hate being shackled to such a boring, thankless task. And if they do take it on they would probably find it hard to resist putting in swirls and flourishes to 'improve' the design, which would then invalidate the test.

In practice, designers are seldom involved in e-commerce optimization as the finished web page is usually done by the developer when they code the split test.

There is a time and a place for outstanding creativity but optimization is not one of them. Occasionally, new icons or graphics need to be created by a design professional but this is rare. Managing your designer's expectations now will help keep team morale high later on.

How big should your team be?

If you are a smaller business, several roles could be taken on by one individual – handling all the research and analysis, setting priorities, project managing the split tests and even doing some copywriting. Larger organizations often have a dedicated project manager and several analysts and developers.

How many people do you need to do CRO? We've seen CRO teams as small as one person and as large as a 40-strong group. You don't necessarily need a big team. That's not what defines success. What's more important is to have the right mindset and to systematically follow a methodology.

You may find that introducing CRO has several unexpected benefits. Many organizations report that CRO and split testing bring people together and help break down silos between departments as everyone works together for a common goal.[2] This process forces everyone to really look at things from a customer perspective and not just pay lip service to being customer-focused.

Gathering evidence with tools

Access to data is crucial to the process because the scientific method is fundamentally evidence-led. This is where a range of tools comes in handy, to help you gather the necessary intelligence.

Some will be embedded in your website by placing a tag in the site code. These tags are typically no more than a few lines of JavaScript, that you'll get from the tool provider. In most cases, you can do this using a tag container with limited technical knowledge. See the box 'Implement tools without IT' for more information on this.

Implement tools without IT

To add tools to your site, you need to install code on your website. However, getting new code installed can sometimes be slow and painful if you have to rely on your IT department or developers.

A better solution is to have your developer do a once-off installation of a tag manager, such as Google Tag Manager (GTM). This is like a holder for CRO tools so in future you can quickly add them without any IT input.

The only tool which you can't put into a tag manager is your split-testing platform. Our recommendation is to avoid using the tag manager and instead place the tag directly in your website code, exactly as instructed by the vendor.

Here is a list of the types of tools, including popular examples of each, that will help you to uncover the best opportunities on your site. How to get the most out of them is discussed over the next few chapters.

Clickstream data

These tools show you what is happening on your website. You can see where visitors came from, what paths they followed on the site, what content they consumed and what products they bought, to mention only a few.

A clickstream tracking tool is essential, because it can help you answer almost any question you have about on-site behaviour. There's a good chance that you already have one and an equally good chance that it's **Google Analytics (GA)**. It has by far the largest market share in this category. This is not surprising: it's free, yet compares well to other solutions for which you have to pay.

Below are some of the most well-known:

Analytics for your mobile app

Many of the tools listed above, including GA, have the ability to track data on mobile apps. Here are some more options:

- Flurry Analytics, free as part of the Yahoo Mobile Developer Suite
- Localytics
- Apsalar
- Appanalytics.io
- Appsee
- Amplitude
- Countly

Table 2.1   Popular clickstream data tracking solutions

Clickstream data tool	Notes
Google Analytics (GA) and Universal Analytics, also by Google	• Used by most websites • Free, powerful, regularly updated • Aggregate data • Can upgrade and pay for premium version for additional functionality such as unsampled reporting and increased data capacity
Kissmetrics	• Marketed as a complement to GA rather than an alternative • Easy to construct finely segmented reports around groups of people that share common characteristics • Strong funnel analysis capabilities, including retrospective funnel visualization, not possible with GA • More advanced cohort analysis than GA
Woopra	• Real-time analytics • Build a single profile for each user by uniting data from your website, mobile apps, CRM, e-mail automation, help desk and other third party services • Advanced segmented funnel reporting
Clicky	• Real-time analytics • Get a detailed granular view of each visitor • Segmented heatmaps • Uptime monitoring
Mixpanel	• Measures actions, rather than page views • Track exactly what people do on your web- or mobile site, or app • Complementary to GA
IBM Analytics	• Enterprise solution • Offers a package tailored to e-commerce
Adobe Analytics	• Enterprise solution • Allows deep segmentation in real time

Behaviour activity maps and session replays

Behaviour activity maps, like heatmaps and scroll maps, show you exactly where your visitors clicked on a page, even when it's not a hyperlink. Session replay tools record short video clips of mouse movements and clicks during visitor sessions that you can play back later.

There is a whole range of vendors you can pick from, each with slightly different features and different price points:

- Clicktale
- Crazy Egg
- Decibel Insight
- Hotjar
- Inspectlet
- Mouseflow
- MouseStats
- Sessioncam

Surveys and polls

Survey data are a vital part of the intelligence gathering process as they let you hear what your visitors and customers think.

Unlike other CRO tools, the software for e-mail surveys is not installed on your website. Instead, you set the survey up in the cloud and then invite people to participate in the survey by sending them a link to it. Companies that offer this service include:

- Client Heartbeat
- Google Consumer Surveys
- Google Forms
- Polldaddy
- Surveygizmo
- Surveymonkey
- Typeform

On-site polls pose questions to your visitors while they are on your site. Some slide in from the bottom of the screen, some have an omni-present button in the corner, while others get activated only when the user's session comes to an end.

Choose a vendor that allows you to select specific segments of visitors. It's a bonus if it can integrate with your split-testing platform, as that could help you to interpret the difference in behaviour between the control and your variation.

Here are some options for running on-site polls at quite different price points:

- Foresee
- Freesurveycreator (free)
- Informizely
- iPerceptions
- Kampyle
- Qeryz
- Qualaroo
- Survicate
- Usabilia
- Webengage

The Swiss Army Knife of CRO

Hotjar is positioned as the 'all in one analytics and feedback' tool. Developed by an experienced optimizer, it combines many of the tools listed above into one package, for example:

- heat- and scroll maps
- session recording
- funnel analysis
- forms analysis
- surveys
- usability testing live recruitment

Being a generalist, it may not be as full featured as the individual tools. Still, it's great if you prefer to get most of your insights in one interface and deal with one vendor only.

Split-testing platform

This mighty tool is the workhorse of your CRO programme. You'll be running a lot of experiments, testing new web pages to find out how your visitors respond to them. A split-test platform lets you do the following:

- serve an alternative version of a webpage or mobile screen to a selection of visitors without needing to touch the code on your main site;
- split traffic to your site so that half of your audience sees the variation and the other half still sees the original. For the visitor, it's a seamless experience so they have no idea they are in a test;
- Calculate how your variation performs against the control and present the results in an easy-to-read dashboard with graphs, tables and reports;
- apply mathematical formulae to determine whether any difference in performance is statistically valid and not just down to random chance.

Even if you have no knowledge of coding, many split-testing platforms offer a drag-and-drop style interface that lets you launch simple experiments. Although that will get you started, especially if you do not have easy access to developers, in the long term you'll be running more sophisticated experiments. These have to be built by someone with knowledge of JavaScript, jQuery and CSS. That's why it's a good idea to have a front-end developer on the team, or to have a reliable firm to outsource.

Below is an overview of popular split-testing vendors:
For larger businesses, the following platforms are popular choices:

- Adobe Test & Target
- Maxymiser
- Monetate
- Qubit
- Sitespect

Summary

To introduce CRO into your organization, first get your team in place. It can be as small as one person aided by ad hoc access to additional resources. Arrange a meeting with all the team members to get the programme off the ground and don't underestimate the importance of a project champion.

Table 2.2   A list of split-testing platforms suitable for small to medium-sized sites

Split-testing platform	Notes
Optimizely	• The world's most popular platform • Founded by former Google executives • Most appropriate for medium-sized or large enterprises and sites with high traffic volumes • Integrates well with third-party tools such as GA, Crazy Egg and Qualaroo • Offers a personalization data layer, sold separately
VWO (formerly known as Visual Website Optimizer)	• Very popular with small to medium-sized businesses • Easy integration with a range of e-commerce platforms including Magento and BigCommerce and various third-party tools • Built-in heatmapping and onsite polling capabilities • Flexible pricing structure
ABTasty	• Most popular in French-speaking countries but gaining traction in the UK and elsewhere
Unbounce	• Focus on mobile-responsive landing pages
Convert.com	• Cheapest package at the time of writing
Hiconversion	• Algorithms adapt to customer preferences in real time
Google Contents Experiment	• Built into GA • Free • Not widely used at the time of writing but there are moves afoot to develop it further, so it's one to watch.

Install research tools on the site to gather information to help you get inside the mind of your customers. Most of them are inexpensive and easy to implement via a tag manager such as GTM.

Choose your split-testing platform. Optimizely and VWO are the market leaders but several others are worth considering too.

Notes

1 Spool, J (2009) The $300 Million Button. Available at: https://articles.uie.com/three_hund_million_button

2 Econsultancy (2014), The Past, Present and Future of Website Optimization

How people buy 03

The research tools are live on your website, ready to start gathering data, and you're about to jump into extensive research and analysis. But, before you start, you should understand just the basics of the psychology of buying – because that's what you'll try to influence.

Later on, as we take you through the whole optimization process, you'll see we refer back to this frequently. It can shape your research efforts and also plays a role in hypothesis development, so understanding how people buy is central to the entire process.

The Conversion Rate metric is black and white. A user has either purchased or not. However, in the mind of the consumer it's not that clear cut. Half-brewed decisions and 'almost bought' moments are strewn along the way; hurdles and interruptions trip the buying brain before making that final decision. To improve your conversion rate, you need to knock down these brain hurdles which means aligning your website with the way the buying brain works.

There is a considerable body of research by behavioural scientists into why people buy, as well as what gets in the way of buying. Optimization aims to change behaviour. Knowledge of relevant behavioural psychology principles helps you do that and also helps you to:

- ask more insightful questions
- formulate better hypotheses to test and
- interpret test results better, to make profitable business decisions.

Why do people buy?

The terms 'shopping' and 'buying' are used interchangeably in everyday conversation but consumer psychologists make a distinction between the two.

Shopping refers to the entire process of going to the store – and its online equivalent – but this doesn't always lead to buying. In fact, 'going shopping' is one of the world's most popular leisure activities, enjoyed for its own sake, regardless of whether anything is purchased.[1] People love shopping so much that it's sometimes known as 'retail therapy' and studies have shown that shopping genuinely does help lift the spirits.

One might think that consuming – that is, using the things that we buy – is what drives us to make a purchase. In reality it's much more complex than that. Author of *Why We Buy*, Paco Underhill, once said, 'If we went into stores only when we needed to buy something, and if once there we bought only what we needed, the economy would collapse – boom.'[2] In other words, we may shop in order to buy stuff but we shop for many other reasons too.

Don't think this is limited to shopping malls and the high street. From our own research done on behalf of many retailers, we have seen that a large portion of mobile phone shopping takes place purely because people are trying to find diversion from everyday tasks such as feeding the baby, cooking dinner and even having work meetings.

What this means for optimization is that your site is likely to have far more visitors who are there to browse than buy. Your objective is to turn more of them into buyers, more frequently, and get them to spend more when they do buy. Understanding the influences that make them purchase during their shopping activity is therefore a central piece in the puzzle.

What makes people buy?

So we know that people shop for different reasons, and that shopping does not always lead to buying. Then what makes them buy?

Often, it is not what it appears to be on the surface, in other words their goal is not directly related to consuming the purchased product.[3] Someone doesn't buy slimming tablets because they want to be taking more pills. Nor even is it to lose weight. No, their goal is seated far deeper – to feel better about themselves.

It's the difference between what you are selling and what your customer is buying. A retailer of outdoor clothing for kids may be selling waterproof coats, but what the mum is buying is the rosy-cheeked smile of her child playing happily in the rain.

Later on in the process, if you have identified that core goal you will be able to adjust the sales messages to resonate with your prospective customer. This is about more than just content; it covers every touch point between your 'online sales team' (your website) and the visitor.

One of our clients is a high-end furniture retailer. When we spoke to their customers about why they bought from this company, no one really mentioned the quality of workmanship: the dovetail joints or the flawless paint finishes. It turns out the reason they bought was because it made them feel special. 'My guests always comment on things I buy from here,' a happy customer said. Her core goal was purely emotional, to be admired for her uniquely stylish taste.

That's why it's so important in e-commerce optimization to be aware of the true reasons why your customers buy and how the decision-making process works. In the situation above it would be easy to fall into the trap of thinking that people would be keen to own these particular home items for the sake of practical utility. That would lead you to follow a feature-driven hard-sell approach which would miss out on so many opportunities to get your site performing to its full potential.

Are you selling to 5 per cent of the brain?

Our brains have two different modes of processing information, known as System 1 (the ancient, unconscious brain) and System 2 (the modern, conscious brain).

One of the best explanations of this is by Nobel Prize winner Daniel Kahneman in his book, *Thinking, Fast and Slow*. He colourfully describes how when we buy anything, these two systems can create internal tension.

Every thought enters the brain via the subconscious System 1, which deals with things automatically and rapidly. Thus the overwhelming majority of thoughts, including purchase decisions, are processed subconsciously. It happens on autopilot, in a flash.

Only about 5 per cent of our decisions and behaviours are escalated to the rational and analytical System 2. This implies that 95 per cent of the time your customers have made their buying decision before they're even aware of it. When conscious thinking takes over, everything gets more complex and nailing a decision becomes difficult. Clearly this is something you want to avoid because it makes people less likely to buy.

If you understand how System 1 and System 2 work, you can use this information to your advantage. At every stage of the optimization process, remember that by the time the conscious mind gets involved, the decision has often already been made.[4] When you get to the point of devising alternative experiences to split test, it may be appropriate to create them to appeal to System 1 thinking. Then, by the time System 2 thinking kicks in, its job is to justify the purchase, rather than putting up intellectual barriers that rationalize against buying.

Table 3.1   The difference between features and benefits, and how it could be expressed

Feature	Benefit	Creative expression
A gadget that grips the lid of a jar to give extra leverage to remove it	Tight jar lids can be removed more easily even by people with a weak grip	Open tight jars in a flash
Spanish learning course	Speaking Spanish quickly and easily	Learn Spanish in your sleep
A doormat that collects dirt from shoes	Floors stay cleaner for longer	Life's too short to mop floors

You will almost certainly have lots of System 2 reasons already to hand as to why your customers should buy from you. The optimization process will help you uncover 'System 1' motivations that you can incorporate into your website.

Roger Dooley, a world-leading neuroscientist, who specializes in retail, strongly advocates leading with content that appeals to System 1's emotional and subconscious needs. That means presenting benefits rather than features. The difference is that features are what a product is or does, while benefits are what it does for the user. Features describe what you are selling – benefits are what the user is really buying.

Sales messages that are dominated by prices, discounts and features tend to tip the balance towards System 2 brain activity.

There is also a difference between the benefit per se and how it is dramatized creatively. Below are three examples to illustrate this.

One retailer who does this well is Zappos, the online shoe store. They use large images on the product detail pages, which trigger an emotional response from System 1. Factual data is placed behind a link, where System 2 can access it to rationalize the purchase decision, but where it's less likely to get in the way of that initial decision.[5]

Six principles of influence

One of the best-known experts on persuasive psychology is Dr Robert Cialdini, author of the chart-topping book, *Influence: The Psychology of Persuasion*. Having studied how to appeal to the subconscious over decades, he offers six ways of getting people 'to say "yes" without thinking first'.[6]

Reciprocation

The rule of reciprocation is so fundamental to the human make-up that it applies to all cultures, all over the world.

Imagine trekking through London's shopping district. It's cold and you're tired from walking around. A store on Regent Street catches your attention. On arrival, the assistant offers you a cup of delicious warm herbal tea. An innocent, generous gesture? Maybe, but there's more to it. That cup is likely to create a feeling of indebtedness towards the shop assistant, easily settled by, well, buying something from the store. This is because the rule of reciprocation asserts that any favour or gift has to be returned. The free unexpected gift is also used by some e-commerce retailers.

An interesting variation of this rule is what Cialdini calls 'rejection-then-retreat'. I recently experienced this when buying a new jacket. The store manager first showed me an enormously expensive jacket. When I made it clear that this was way beyond my budget, he didn't skip a beat and quickly emerged with a similar item about half the price. What a deal! Psychologically, because the second price appears to be small in comparison with the first one, the shopper reacts favourably. This is also known as price anchoring.

Commitment and consistency

Once we've committed to doing something, we face internal and societal tension if we don't see it through. To avoid that, we have an innate drive to be consistent with earlier actions and decisions.

You can use this to your advantage in surprisingly subtle ways. For example if you want someone to fill in an online form, initially you may just ask for some small piece of information such as a name or e-mail address. The theory is that, once they've started the process by giving you that data, they've made a commitment and will be more willing to give much more extensive information later.

Another example is requesting a catalogue on a retailer's website, which leads to the expectation of buying something from that catalogue.

Social Proof

We tend to look at the actions of others for clues on how we should behave. In situations where there's any uncertainty, we are especially likely to copy their behaviour.

Figure 3.1   The social proof message that led to a 6 per cent increase in Revenue Per Visitor

So powerful is this mechanism that it has been employed to cure a fear of dogs in children. Cialdini explains how researchers showed them clips of other kids playing with dogs. Within four days of watching the videos, two thirds of them were petting the same dogs they were previously scared of.

This is one of the most commonly applied techniques in e-commerce. Examples include testimonials, highlighting best sellers and showing the number of Facebook likes. We find comfort in the knowledge that others are there with us, or have trodden the path before us. Hence the saying 'safety in numbers'.

This principle came into play in one project we ran for a large website selling flowers. Adding a simple banner stating 'Over 10 Million Bouquets Delivered' produced an increase of 6 per cent in Revenue Per Visitor. Our research had pointed to a lack of familiarity with the brand being a barrier to buying. The banner gave people the social proof they needed that many others trust the brand, and thus made them feel it was a legitimate site and safe to order from.

Liking

We tend to buy from those we like. One perhaps slightly controversial method cited by Cialdini is showing photographs of attractive people. Only if it's relevant to your product, I should add.

You can invoke liking by creating the suggestion of similarity. We want to associate with people like us. One way to do this would be to carefully select testimonials to align with your target personas. Some e-commerce sites have even used the old boring About Us page to introduce liking, by depicting the team as friendly, honest people – just like you and me.

Authority

We are easily influenced by authority figures, especially those with credentials such as 'doctor', 'professor', etc. Influence can also be achieved by quoting from authoritative sources, for example, citing studies, showing excerpts from academic journals or even just a photograph of someone in a white coat.

Scarcity

Things tend to increase in value as supply is lessened. So we are more likely to buy something if stock is low. This is a frequently encountered tactic on e-commerce sites and is partly behind the psychology of 'daily deals' sites.

Bonus: the rule of material self-interest

People want to maximize gains and minimize cost, in other words they want to get the most for the lowest possible price. This seventh principle is given only scant attention by Cialdini in his foreword, explaining that it is such an obvious factor that it was deliberately omitted from the official list.

Lowest price does not always mean cheapest and it's not always monetary value alone that's important but the whole experience. The perception of a good deal often counts for more than the actual price.

In fact, when we spot something we want for a lot less than expected, our brains light up with pleasure in exactly the same place as when people take heroin, according to research by Dr David Lewis.[7] When it comes to snapping up a bargain, it seems we just can't resist.

The consumer buying decision-making process

An e-commerce transaction doesn't start, or end for that matter, with a purchase. The purchase is the only visible link in a chain of events that starts much earlier, and continues beyond the point where the transaction is concluded. The buying decision-making process[8] is a well-known framework that shows the mental stages consumers pass through when buying products:

- Need recognition
- Information search
- Evaluation of alternatives
- Purchase of product
- Post-purchase evaluation

Figure 3.2 The consumer buying decision-making process shows the various mental stages involved in making a purchase

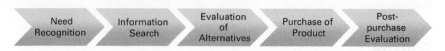

Need recognition

Without a need, there can't be a purchase. Not only that but it influences everything around the purchase decision and even satisfaction levels after purchase. This is why it's so crucial to really understand your customer's core need, which is what large parts of the next chapters are devoted to.

Information search

Once the need is recognized, consumers search for information about potential solutions. They might do a Google search, ask friends for recommendations, or look at customer reviews. Purchases of everyday goods also pass through this step but we tend to use memory recall or previous experience to find the information.

With tools like Google Analytics, it's possible to see what search terms visitors used to find your site. You may observe that some phrases relate to early exploratory stages, while others are closer to the next step of evaluating alternatives.

Evaluation

Having completed their information search, your potential customer now has a range of possibilities. It may amount to nothing but price comparison, which is so easy online. In that case, you have to justify your prices, if you aren't the lowest in the market. Key here is your value proposition, which we discuss in Chapter 5.

One of our clients is a famous electronic goods brand. The major sales objection on their website is that the same products can be bought at prices up to 20 per cent less from popular retail outlets. Our research revealed that their customers were prepared to pay more for the promise of global warranties, availability of the full product range and a fear of buying inferior 'grey' imports from department stores. That knowledge enabled us to mirror it back at visitors, boosting their perception of value.

Figure 3.3   Evaluating alternatives

SOURCE   Image courtesy of Dunelm PLC

Other factors that can help consumers narrow down options include product attributes and brand perception. Different attributes appeal to different people. You may think you know what matters to customers but it's always worth checking this with surveys. Brand perception is a subjective judgement based on things such as the look and feel of your site or the content and tone of your messages. Be sensitive to that when creating alternative designs to split test.

In Figure 3.3: the client, a famous retail chain, makes the evaluation of alternatives easier by offering a great variety of product images. This invokes System 1 thinking by subtly answering key questions that a customer may have. What is the shape? How thick is it? How large is it? What is the texture like? These can all be answered subconsciously by looking at this collection of images. By the time the user examines the product copy, it may be just a matter of System 2 rationalizing the decision, already made subconsciously by then.

Purchase

Finally, we get to the source of that metric so keenly tracked, conversion rate. Hopefully this discussion helps to put it in context and underscores the importance of investigating what happens 'upstream'. However, just because a potential customer made a choice at the Evaluation stage, there is no guarantee they will conclude the transaction. Some evidence of this can be seen in the high percentage of baskets that get abandoned – an average of around 68 per cent across the board at the time of writing.[9]

Post-purchase behaviour

After making the purchase, your customer evaluates to what extent the product meets their original need. Whether or not those expectations are met determines customer satisfaction. In some cases the consumer will do another round of Information search, this time to confirm that they've made the right decision. In behavioural psychology this is known as an attempt to reduce post-purchase cognitive dissonance – or buyer's remorse, which is surprisingly common. What they experience at this point can influence future sales.

FBM Model of behaviour

Now that we've examined the decision-making process that precedes action, it's time to take a closer look at the action component itself. What makes people take a desired action, such as buying a product from your site?

Dr BJ Fogg of Stanford University shed light on this question with the Fogg Behavioural Model (FBM). It does a great job of capturing the fundamentals of complex human behaviour. For any given behaviour to occur, three things need to fall into place at the same time: motivation, ability and trigger.

- Motivation refers to how strongly the individual is driven to act. Ability relates to how easy it is for that individual to take the desired action, ie usability in our context.

- Theoretically, an individual who is low on motivation can be converted by increasing motivation. While in practice this is not easy, it emphasizes the importance of understanding your customer's motivation.

Figure 3.4   The Fogg Behavioural Model shows how different factors come together to make target behaviour occur

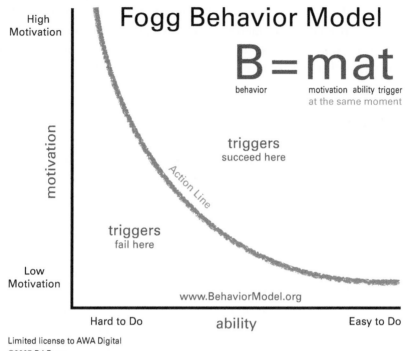

Limited license to AWA Digital
©2007 BJ Fogg

- Studies have shown that highly motivated users actually underestimate usability difficulties.[10] Therefore, someone with high motivation may be influenced to act by improving usability. It's one of the most effective interventions. A good way to identify these opportunities is by doing remote moderated usability testing, covered in Chapter 4.

- Your visitor will not take action without a trigger, even when motivation and ability are both high. Consequently, this is an area you want to be paying attention to. If the need is strong enough, it could act as a trigger. More tangible examples are e-mails with discount codes and the offer of free delivery above a certain basket value. How about your calls to action? Is the button visible? Does the copy resonate with the user's need? Are you infusing triggers with benefits and features, when an appeal to System 1 thinking would be more appropriate?

- Timing is everything, according to Fogg. A trigger at a time when either motivation or ability is low will not result in a sale. All three ingredients have to come together, at the same time, for the credit card number to be punched in.

FBM in practice

Samantha has been eyeing a great-looking office dress on the website of a fashion retailer. She's even been into the store to try it on. It's perfect ... but expensive. So, there's some motivation to buy it, the ability is there, but the trigger is missing. One day she's invited to an exciting job interview. She wants to look her best. Suddenly, timing is right. Ker-ching!

Summary

Your task as an optimizer is to influence behaviour. A basic understanding of relevant behavioural psychology principles will serve you well as you go through the optimization process.

It will shape your analysis, help you formulate better hypotheses and improve your interpretation of the outcome of split tests. You'll be a better optimizer and get better results.

We tend to view buying as a simple yes/no decision. In fact, it's not black and white, but several shades of grey. About 95 per cent of all decisions happen subconsciously. This means that we tend to purchase with emotion more than rational deliberation – even if we think we don't.

As a consequence, throughout your optimization process, you should be trying to identify the core needs and motivations of your target customers so that you can align your approach with that.

The FBM model explains that motivation alone is not enough to make someone buy. There must also be a trigger and ability, which means that if you want more sales, then you need to make buying easy.

Notes

1 Lewis, D (2013) *The Brain Sell: When science meets shopping*, Nicholas Brealey Publishing, London.

2 Underhill, P (2008) *Why We Buy: The science of shopping*, Simon & Schuster, New York.

3 Ratneshwar, S, David Mick and Cynthia Huffman (2000) *The Why of Consumption: Contemporary perspectives on consumer motives, goals and desires*, Routledge, New York.

4 Lewis, D (2013) *The Brain Sell: When science meets shopping*, Nicholas Brealey Publishing, London.

5 Dooley, Roger (2012) *Brainfluence: 100 ways to persuade and convince consumers with neuromarketing*, John Wiley & Sons Inc, Hoboken.

6 Cialdini, Robert (2007) *Influence: The psychology of persuasion*, p xiv, Harper Collins, New York.

7 Lewis, D (2013) *The Brain Sell: When science meets shopping*, Nicholas Brealey Publishing, London.

8 Blackwell, R D, Miniard, P W and Engel, J F (2005) *Consumer Behavior*, 10th edn, South-Western College Pub, Mason, OH.

9 Baymard Institute (2016) 33 cart abandonment rate statistics. Available at: http://baymard.com/lists/cart-abandonment-rate (accessed: 1 July 2016).

10 Venkatesh, V (2000) Determinants of perceived ease of use: integrating control, intrinsic motivation, and emotion into the technology acceptance model. Information Systems Research, 11(4), 342–365.

Essential research

04

You may have an idea already of what to change on your site to improve performance but no one person can be expected to know all the problems – and have all the answers. You also have a finite number of split tests that you can run in a given period, so you want to make the most of each one.

To get a steer on where you should be focusing your efforts, we turn to research and analysis. It will give you confidence in deciding what to test and the order in which to test them. It also keeps things objective and gives you ammunition to politely counter subjective opinions.

The research landscape

Qualitative versus quantitative research

One of the most common ways of thinking about research is to split it up into qualitative and quantitative methods. Quantitative research tells you *what* is happening whereas qualitative research helps explain *why* it is happening. In broad terms, qualitative is what people say and quantitative is about numbers. However, these are not mutually exclusive as many research techniques have elements of both.

In e-commerce optimization, the research technique you would choose depends on the type of insight you hope to gain. The value of qualitative research is in discovery and exploration. Use it to find ideas that can inform hypotheses directly, or sparks that you can develop further with other forms of research.

So, qualitative is useful for generating insights. To be sure they are representative they should be of a wider audience, and to know whether it's really important in the bigger scheme of things, you would back it up with quantitative data.

Attitudinal versus behavioural insights

To build a view of your users, you need different types of insight. Aim for a balance of data between attitudinal (what people believe and say) and behavioural (what they do). Interviews and surveys are great ways to learn about the goals and attitudes of users. However, humans are notoriously poor at predicting their own behaviour.

For behavioural insights, it's better to observe people in a situation rather than asking them how they'd react in that scenario. Asking users how to improve a page is asking them to predict their behaviour – they can't. Steve Jobs famously said: 'A lot of times, people don't know what they want until you show it to them.'[1] But what they can tell you about is the teeth-gnashing frustration they feel when they can't do something quickly and easily on the site.

Figure 4.1   The e-commerce optimization research landscape

SOURCE Adapted from Mulder, S (2006) *The User is Always Right: A practical guide to creating and using personas for the web*, New Riders, Berkeley

Below are some of the most valuable research techniques you'll learn about over the next two chapters, mapped out to show what type of insight they are best for.

Personas

Surrounded by masses of data, it's easy to lose sight of the fact that behind all the data are real people – your site visitors and customers. Yet, anything that appears on a web page is ultimately there to try and get human beings to take a certain action. It follows that you have to understand who those people are. What are their interests, needs and pain points? What motivates them to buy?

Personas can help you to get a handle on that. A persona is a character who represents an archetypal user. Though fictional, they should be firmly based on data and grounded in reality. Personas remind you that you are not optimizing for yourself, but for a user. You are not your user. Your boss is not your user. The UX-consultant is not your user.

Many well-publicized optimization methodologies lack this component, which we regard as an oversight. Some practitioners write personas off as a bit woolly, and Jason Fried of 37signals may have spoken on behalf of many others when he dismissed personas as 'artificial, abstract, and fictitious'.[2] Indeed, if your personas are born in a brainstorming session, without much user data, they're pointless. However, if you base them on actual people, if they are informed by research, they can be immensely useful. In fact, a study found that the use of personas led to superior user experience in design.[3]

When you create a wireframe with one person in mind, or when you rewrite a product description to talk directly to that person, it brings clarity and focus. A key persona for one of our clients is Julia, based on real interviews we conducted with mothers of young babies. In the early hours of the morning, in a quiet part of the house away from the rest of the family, she is feeding her baby. Julia is based on several customers who described to us how they would start browsing our client's mobile site, making mental notes of things to come back to later. Do you think that a wireframe designed with her in mind looks different from one without this vision of Julia? Absolutely.

What does a persona look like?

The essence of persona creation is described by Alan Cooper, a pioneer of the method: 'Develop a precise description of your user and what they wish to accomplish.'[4] Fundamentally, that boils down to two things: a biography of sorts plus a goal statement.

Cooper emphasized that goals and personas are two sides of the same coin. It's easy to fall into the trap of focusing too much on the person, and not enough on goals. To avoid that, think of your product as something that the customer 'hires' to get a particular job done.[5] This is the essence of a framework known as Jobs To Be Done (JTBD), which helps you to think about your user's core goal, which might be something like:

- Impress guests with exclusive, expensive wine
- Encourage young child to read by buying story books
- Let my wife know I'm thinking of her by sending her some flowers

The third vital component of personas is scenarios; stories that outline the sequence of activities carried out by the user to achieve their goal. The biographical content varies depending on your context. Unless demographics are central to your business model, it doesn't have to take centre stage in your personas. Don't neglect it though, as it serves to complete the narrative and make the persona real and memorable. For the same reason, your persona should be polished with a name and, preferably, even a face.

Figure 4.2   Personas should be goal-driven and focused on motivations

---

Harry

Job: Software Engineer
Location: London
Age: 28

Goals and Motivations:

- Works long hours and wants to have better work-life balance
- Likes the idea of being barefoot in nature, but not the thorns

Scenario:

- Reads about the concept of barefoot shoes in a blog
- Conducts a Google search for 'barefoot shoes'
- Looks at three different competitor websites
- Compares features and prices of shoes
- Reads several customer reviews
- Opts for a running sandal that suits his style

SOURCE LukaFunduk/DepositPhotos

How to create personas

Whatever you do, don't brainstorm them from your own assumptions about users. Useful personas are not fabricated, but discovered through analysis. A strong research bedrock is what makes them credible.

Focus your personas on core motivations. What do they want to achieve by buying the product? How do they want their lives to improve, or be different, as a result of buying the product?

Nothing beats semi-structured interviews for learning about your users' needs, goals, motivations, behaviours and attitudes. Visiting users at their home or office provides a richer experience but telephone interviews are easier and more cost-effective. Allow the conversation to unfold naturally and let the interviewee do most of the talking. Stick to open-ended questions and ask only one question at a time. Other valuable data sources are e-mail and onsite surveys, as well as moderated user testing. Below is a list of sample questions:

Context

- Tell us a bit about yourself.
- How did you first become aware of the site/product? Describe the circumstances.
- What was your first interaction with the brand? Store, computer, mobile device, call centre, app, catalogue, etc?
- Where were you when you first/last visited the site?
- How often do you buy online?
- What is your favourite shopping site?
- What is your favourite non-shopping site?

Needs

- What exactly was it that prompted you to visit the site the first time?
- What has made you come back to the site?
- Which competitors would you consider?
- Why exactly did you need the product that you came to the site for?
- At the time of buying the product, what difference did you think it would make in your life?

Goals

- How would your life be different without this product?
- When you first visited the site, what was it that you wanted to do?
- Did you manage to achieve that goal? If not, why not?
- What did you want to do on subsequent visits? On your most recent visit?
- When you last visited the site of a competitor, what was it that you wanted to do? Did you manage to achieve that goal? If not, why not?
- What would you like to be able to do on this site, but can't?
- How are you using the product?
- Are you using feature X of product Y?

Motivations

- What will make you visit the site more frequently?
- Describe the decision-making process when you made your last purchase on the site or that of a competitor.
- Did you have any doubts or fears about buying on the site?
- What was it that persuaded you to buy from us the first time/last time?
- What was it that persuaded you to buy from a competitor instead?
- What has stopped you buying from our site or that of a competitor?

Attitudes

- What were your first impressions about the brand/site? How has that view changed over time?
- How would you describe this brand/site to a friend?
- What do you like about competitors and their sites?
- How does this site compare with the competitor's?
- If you were CEO and could do anything, what changes would you make to the site? Why?
- If this site disappeared today, how would it affect you? What would you use instead?

Behaviours

- What is the dominant channel of interaction with the brand? Store, computer, mobile device, call centre, app, etc.
- How often do you visit this site?
- How often do you visit the site of a competitor?
- When last did you visit this site or that of a competitor?
- Think back to your last visit to the site. Describe your journey.
- Describe a typical journey on this site.
- Describe a typical journey on a competitor's site.

How many personas do you need?

Each persona represents a different customer segment. Segment by goals or behaviour, rather than demographics. If you aren't sure at this stage what those segments should be, don't let it distract you. Start interviewing. Soon enough, it will become clear and you'll see personas taking shape naturally. You can kick-start the process with an internal brainstorm, but don't let fictional pen portraits created out of uninformed beliefs stop you putting together well-researched personas.

Some experts recommend creating a persona for each segment across the entire spectrum, including ones you don't cater for. That is boiling the ocean in our view. One primary persona and around three to four secondary personas should suffice in most cases. The exact number is not important, as long as you have covered the key ones for your situation.

Aim for at least five interviews per persona. In our experience, this is enough to provide depth and colour alongside your quantitative data. As you're gathering the data, start breaking it into themes. Look out for patterns and commonalities that you can base the different personas on.

User journey mapping

Your visitors leave behind trails of data that you can use to plot their paths through the site. Along with personas, journey mapping forms the ideal backdrop to the rest of your research. In fact, many e-commerce marketers say that journey mapping is their single most valuable tool.[6] A visualization of this data, as shown in Figure 4.3, gives you a great behavioural overview and exposes leaks in the funnel quickly. This often highlights areas for further investigation, and might give you an early steer on potential opportunities.

A segmented view is always more meaningful than just looking at one block of aggregate data. The example in Figure 4.3 shows segmentation by device category. What jumps out at you? Certainly, the comparatively large drop-off on the basket page for mobile devices should prompt further examination. There are many ways to slice the data, eg geographic, behaviour and acquisition source. Examining the differences between converting and non-converting segments can also be instructive. Think about what is most relevant for your particular context.

On the face of it, the Product Detail Pages (PDPs) seem to present a massive opportunity in this example. It's worth noting that PDPs usually tend to have a high drop-off rate, especially on sites with large product ranges. Why? If you think back to the consumer decision-making model from Chapter 3, it's natural for people to look at products without buying, often several times. Before they buy they're searching for solutions, evaluating alternatives, doing price comparisons and they even come back to it after the purchase.

How to create a customer journey

First, scope the funnel. This means identifying the key pages that represent steps in your user journey. A typical e-commerce funnel looks something like this:

Visitors → Category Page → Product Listing Page (PLP) → Product
Detail Page (PDP) → Add to Cart → Basket → Checkout → Sale

Use Google Analytics (GA) to count the number of unique visitors to each step in the journey. There are many different ways in which to access this data. Our preference is to create a new dashboard, adding a widget for each step of the journey. If pages aren't already grouped in GA, use regex (you'll find helpful tools online) to combine them into one step. Once you've created a widget for each major step in the funnel, you can easily segment the data and then export it into Excel for analysis.

Use an extended time frame to account for seasonal differences. A full year is a good guideline. Segment the data by device category, converters versus non-converters and any other grouping relevant to your context. All that remains then is to calculate the drop-off rate between different steps and present it in an easy-to-understand visual.

The top line of the diagram below shows a typical visitor journey as they go from one type of page to another in an e-commerce site. Underneath shows how many people drop out at each stage, segmented by the device used.

GA segmentation and advanced segments

Incidentally, whatever GA reports you use, nothing is more important than segmenting that data. Analytics guru Avinash Kaushik doesn't mince his words: 'no segments, no insights, no job.'[7]

Why they are so vital is clearly illustrated in Figure 4.3. Take a closer look at the drop-off rates between the basket page and the login page. Overall, 21 per cent of users are lost here, but we can see that most of that leakage comes from mobile users (30 per cent) and tablet users (34 per cent). Only 8 per cent of desktop users are lost, which highlights the need to improve the experience on handheld devices.

GA gives you several options for segmentation. Two popular ones are inline segments and advanced segments.

Inline segments

This is a quick 'on-the-fly' method of segmenting. In the example below, we have broken the Landing Pages report down by adding *Source/Medium* as a secondary dimension. This will show the various traffic sources for each page.

Advanced segments

An optimizer's best friend! Unlike inline segmentation, advanced segments are applied at a global level. As the name suggests, you can really dig deep and use this feature to answer almost any question as long as the key drivers are tracked in GA. The list of possible advanced segments is practically infinite, but here are some examples:

- Desktop/mobile visitors who bought more than x times
- Visitors who spent between x and y
- Visitors who came from Facebook and whose first session was on x date
- Customers who bought product x after seeing page y
- Paid Search traffic who saw advertisement x and then added a product to cart

In the example below we are creating a segment for users who purchased furniture, by specifying the relevant product categories where prompted.

Figure 4.3 An example of a customer journey map, segmented by device

Drop-off rate by device

	Visits	Category	Product	Add to basket	Basket	Login/ Sign In	Delivery	Payment	Order Confirm
All	0%	42%	91%	33%	21%	5%	3%	11%	
Desktop	0%	37%	91%	36%	8%	4%	4%	10%	
Tablet	0%	37%	91%	27%	34%	5%	1%	16%	
Mobile	0%	60%	93%	32%	30%	10%	2%	17%	

Figure 4.4 Segmenting data in GA by using inline segmentation

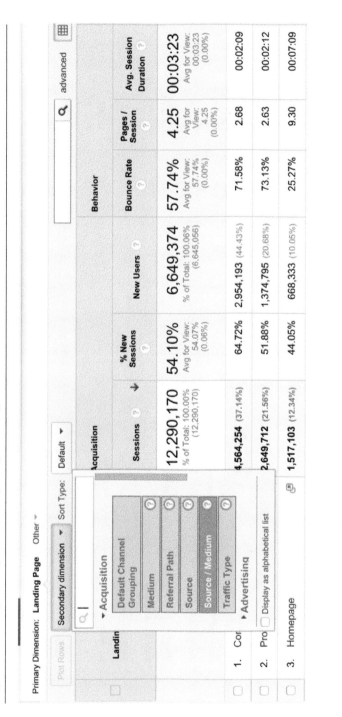

Figure 4.5 Example of an advanced segment in Google Analytics – a powerful feature

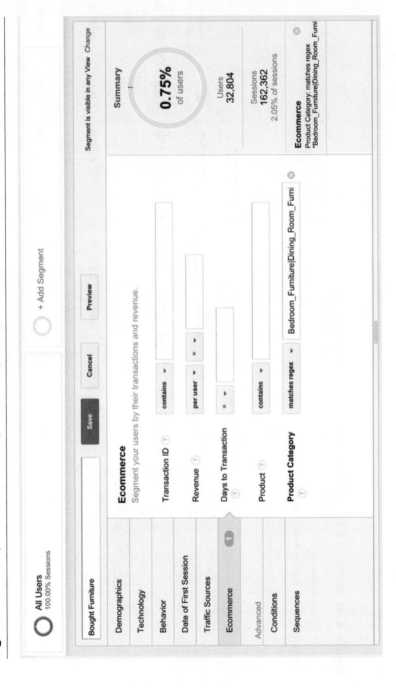

You can make up your own custom segments by mixing and matching various attributes associated with demographics, technology, behaviour and more. This is then available for you to use as an advanced segment to apply to almost any report. For example, we could then create a journey map for only those visitors who bought furniture by applying this advanced segment to our dashboard.

Usability testing

Once you know where visitors are leaking out of your funnel, you can start thinking about plugging those leaks. But that alone is not enough – you should want to explore why those areas are weaker. It's time to fill in the gaps with qualitative research.

Imagine the knowledge you would gain if you could be a fly on the wall when a visitor is using your site, especially if you could somehow hear what they were thinking at the same time. It would give you a great insight into the confusion and anxieties that are blocking conversions.

This is exactly what usability testing (or user testing) is – observing users interacting with your site or app while verbalizing their thoughts. If done properly, it's like getting totally under the skin and into the mind of your users. This is important, because as an optimizer, you don't move things around on a page to make it look pretty, even if that is a secondary outcome. Primarily, you remove obstacles in the conversion path and introduce changes which influence user behaviour.

There are different ways in which to approach this.

Remote user testing

At one time, most user testing was done in a laboratory. Research subjects would take time out of their day to visit the lab and conduct the test, while being observed from behind one-way glass. It was hugely expensive as well as being an artificial environment, which may cause users to behave differently from how they would at home.

Nowadays, it's easy to do user testing remotely, without the need for a specialized lab environment. Quite literally, you can be on the other side of the world, talking to a customer, in their home, watching how they use your site.

Remote usability studies can be facilitated by a moderator or be unmoderated. Let's look at the difference.

Unmoderated user testing

Unmoderated testing is quick and inexpensive thanks to automated platforms like usertesting.com, whatusersdo.com, Loop11, usersthink.com, userlytics and trymyui.com. Typically lasting just a few minutes per session, participants log in from their own home at a time of their choosing and carry out specific tasks, speaking their thoughts out loud. Their voice and all on-screen activities are recorded for you to watch later.

Setting the tasks

At the start of your user-testing session give the participant tasks to perform. Preferably, these are linked to the goals that you identified in persona development.

The nature of this type of research lends itself to getting both qualitative and quantitative feedback around specific questions. Looking back at Figure 4.3, for example, we might ask: 'What percentage of users encounter problems at this point?' (quantitative) or 'Why is there such a comparatively high basket abandonment on handheld devices?' (qualitative).

To find out, you need to set a task that would enable you to observe that specific behaviour. Usability expert Jakob Nielsen offers the following guidelines for setting meaningful tasks:[8]

- Set the task in a scenario, rather than issuing a blunt instruction without any context. So rather than just 'Buy a bunch of flowers', say, 'Imagine that it's your mum's birthday tomorrow and you want to have flowers delivered to her house. Visit my-flowers-site.com and choose something that you think your mum would like.'

- Keep it realistic for the user. The example above is not too prescriptive about either the item to be purchased, or amount to be spent. This gives the user the freedom to adapt the task to their circumstances and encourages natural behaviour. Asking someone to buy a particular bouquet in this case would have been the wrong approach. It may be that a user dislikes that type of flowers and would never buy them in real life.

- Make it actionable. Don't ask users what they would do. Ask them to do it. Continuing the example from above, we wouldn't ask them to talk us through what they would buy and where they would click.

- Don't explain the process in too much detail or list the steps to be followed as this could give them clues on what to do. Since they don't have that benefit in real life, your usability problems may not come to light. Instead of 'Add the item/s to your basket, then click on the green button at the bottom of the screen', simply state: 'Proceed to buy the item/s.'

Selecting your participants

Finding people to test is easy when you use automated user-testing platforms, with vast and ever-growing networks of testers ready and willing to take part. Be warned though that this can be a double-edged sword: those testers are not necessarily representative of your visitors and customers. Many panellists are doing it semi-professionally, which can result in responses coming across as predictable and rehearsed. Some panels seem to attract individuals from a design or UX background who can't resist giving best practice advice, rather than reflecting on their own individual experience.

You can mitigate against this by defining the profile of respondents carefully. If possible, don't rely only on basic demographic profiling but use custom questions to screen them. If your target is mothers of young children, like our persona Julia from earlier, you could ask a custom question such as 'Do you have any children under the age of two?' You can also use these questions to filter out undesirable tester profiles, for example, 'Do you have a background in design or UX?'

Moderated user testing

As the name suggests, moderated user testing refers to the study being conducted in the presence of a facilitator. Instead of the user completing the tasks on their own, they do it while you are watching. It can be done in person, at your office for example, or remotely using simple technology – nothing more than a phone and screen-sharing tools like GoToMeeting, JoinMe and Adobe Connect. You could even consider Skype and Google Hangouts although both require accounts and may be a barrier for some as these tools can represent personal space.

The advantage of a moderated approach is the ability to interact with your tester and ask follow up questions, like 'what did you mean by that?' or 'could you say a bit more about why you think that?' It allows you to explore unexpected paths, which can be extremely valuable.

This 'go with the flow' aspect has led to some of our greatest insights and discoveries. During one study, for a well-known bakery chain, the moderator observed that the user was struggling to carry out the task of ordering fresh cakes from the website. The moderator gently explored why this was, being careful not to give specific instructions like 'why don't you click there?'

Eventually the user remarked: 'What?! You mean I can actually order these cakes online and have them delivered to me?' At this point, it dawned on the moderator that despite lots of visual clues, such as a basket icon and banners about delivery, it had not even occurred to the user that it was possible to buy fresh cakes online. It seemed obvious to the client, but was clearly not obvious to all users.

This was an *aha* moment that would not have surfaced in an unmoderated setting. It also required the researcher to recognize it as a valuable insight and not dismiss the tester as an idiot. This casual remark was developed into the hypothesis that sales would go up if more visitors were made aware that they could buy from the site.

A simple experiment was developed in which everything was the same as before, apart from an additional headline on the homepage saying 'Shop online now – from our bakery to your door'. These nine words delivered an 18 per cent increase in Revenue Per Visitor.

Recruiting your testers

To recruit people for usability testing, we recommend that you intercept users on your site as they are actually using it. This allows you to observe a truly authentic experience. Known as live recruiting, there are several tools you can use, but one of our favourites is Ethnio. It serves a pop-up to users like the one below and when someone responds, you can call them immediately and conduct the research right there and then.

It is always preferable to source research subjects from your own site, ideally in real time. However, if that's not possible, then you can reach out to your database by e-mail or telephone. Regardless of the method you use, it's a good idea to offer a small incentive, such as a gift voucher. It will increase your response rate and it's also fair to thank people and compensate them for their time. Detractors of this say that it can skew the results but it's still better than not having any data.

How to do it

With live recruiting, once you've found a participant, phone them up right away and direct them to the screen-sharing facility. Ask them to continue the session as though you weren't there. I can't stress enough the importance of having them speak their thoughts out loud. Your role then is to observe, listen and take notes.

When they go quiet, give them a gentle nudge eg 'what are you looking at now?' or 'is this what you were expecting to see?' Apart from that, keep

Figure 4.6 Example of a pop-up served by Ethnio to recruit usability testers in real time

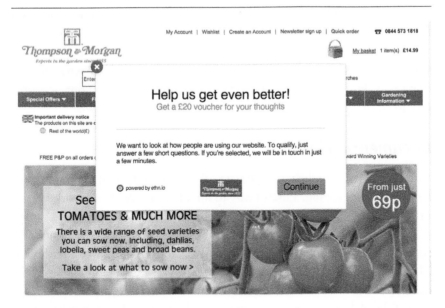

SOURCE Image courtesy of Ethnio

quiet and let them get on with it. Resist the temptation to tell them how to do it, especially if they get stuck. Rather let that one individual struggle, even if it means losing a sale, so that you can see what's going wrong and fix it for everyone else.

If they ask you questions, throw it back at them. For example, if someone wants to know how to proceed to checkout, you could ask: 'what do you think you should do next?' Giving them any directions kills your opportunity to learn.

Documenting insights

Summarize your findings as you go. Whether you do unmoderated or moderated user testing, a useful way to do it is in a spreadsheet with a separate row for each observation. Then create a column for each user.

Rank each observation in terms of severity as H (High), M (Medium) or L (Low). H is a showstopper. The user is unlikely to continue beyond this point. M means something gets in the way of a motivated user, almost preventing the sale. L is a minor irritation but the conversion is not jeopardized.

In Table 4.1, only User 1 encountered Observation 1, a minor irritation. Observation 2 was encountered by both User 1 and User 3, but it affected them in different ways as reflected by the severity scores.

For each observation, count the number of times it appears in user columns and label it 'Occurrence'. In this way, you can measure how often you observed that particular behaviour, frustration, blockage or other issue. The more frequent an observation and the higher its severity, the more urgent it is to look into.

How many users do you need?

The number of sessions that you need to get relevant insights has long been debated. An often-quoted statistic comes from the seminal work of Jakob Nielsen and Tom Landauer.[9] They found that just five testers reveal 85 per cent of a site's usability problems, after which the law of diminishing returns sets in.

Table 4.1   A basic log for capturing observations in usability testing

	User 1	User 2	User 3
Observation 1	L		
Observation 2	L		H
Observation 3		M	

We have found this rule of thumb to hold good for most projects. The only caveat is when you have two or more distinct groups of users. In that case include representatives from each group and aim to test three or four users per group.

A last word on usability testing: it's good to do follow-up studies throughout the optimization lifecycle as you make improvements to the site. At the very least it may validate some of your interventions, but invariably fresh opportunities will emerge.

E-mail surveys

An e-mail survey is a great way of getting to know your users quickly, because it's easy to launch and can generate a large number of responses. Use it to gather demographic and attitudinal data across a broad spectrum, but acknowledge that it's not great at exposing usability problems.

Open or closed questions?

A survey is only as good as the questions. We tend to prefer open-ended questions and open text responses. This is to avoid leading the respondent into an answer and to benefit from hearing the respondent's own words. Sometimes the way in which something is expressed, or the specific words chosen, are as important as what is being said. This is lost when respondents are given answers to choose from.

These responses can also help you later on with creative work, because the actual quotes can be valuable to inform copy and may even end up

Table 4.2 Codifying open-text responses for quantitative analysis

What convinced you to buy from us as opposed to a competitor?				
Special offer	**Price**	**Range**	**Quality**	**Loyalty**
1	0	0	1	0
0	1	1	0	0
0	1	1	0	1
1	0	0	0	0
1	0	0	0	0
0	0	1	1	0
1	1	0	0	0
0	1	1	0	0

being used semi-verbatim in copy or headlines. Although primarily a qualitative research technique, it's possible to apply quantitative analysis to open-question analysis, provided you have sufficient responses, as shown below.

There is however the advantage, with closed questions, of changing the direction of questions depending on the responses given, a technique known as conditional branching. This way you can have respondents self-select their segment, and then ask them relevant follow-up questions. Some examples of segments that we use regularly include:

- one-time buyers
- multi-buyers
- non-buyers
- lapsed buyers
- big spenders

How many questions should you ask in a survey?

There are no hard and fast rules about the ideal number of questions. Nevertheless, always pose as few as you possibly can, especially if you use open text. Give the option to skip questions unless you have a good reason to make it mandatory such as 'conditional branching questions' where you need a response in order to channel the respondent down the appropriate path.

Sample questions

What questions to ask depends on so many things that it's impossible to offer a universal list. The following, together with those presented earlier in this chapter, are just meant to give you ideas. Think about your unique situation and what you need to know about your customers and their needs.

Closed questions:
- Demographics: age, education, etc.
- How many times have you bought from our online shop?
  - never
  - in the last 30 days
  - 1–3 months ago
  - more than 3 months ago

- How often do you visit our site to look at an item but go into one of our stores to buy it?
  - not usually
  - sometimes
  - routinely

- How would you describe yourself?
  - professional photographer
  - serious amateur
  - novice

- Do you:
  - own your house?
  - rent your house?

- What products have you purchased from our site?
- How frequently do you purchase X product?
- When last did you purchase from us?

Open or closed, depending on your objectives and existing intelligence. If closed, always offer an 'Other, please specify' option:

- What alternative products/technologies did you consider before buying this item?
- At which shops or online stores have you shopped for the product you most recently purchased from our site?
- What factors did you consider when buying the product you most recently purchased from our site?
- Which website do you like buying from?
- What is it about your favourite shopping site that you like?

Open text answers, where the purpose is to get attitudinal insight:

- How would you describe our site/product/brand to a friend?
- What influenced your decision to purchase online as opposed to instore?
- Why did you buy from us and not another website or shop?
- What do you like about Competitor X?
- What do you like about us compared with Competitor X?

- What has been the best/worst thing about your experience as our customer?

- What concerns and fears did you have when shopping on our site?

- What one thing could we change to persuade you to shop with us more?

- Please describe your entire decision-making process behind your most recent purchase. For example: I was looking for blinds, but didn't want to pay too much, and a friend recommended your brand. I had a look online and was impressed with the prices. I visited one of your stores to look at the blinds, then went home to order online.

- How are you using product X?

- Why exactly did you need the product that you came to the site for?

- It can be said that we buy things to improve aspects of our lives. What difference in your life did you *expect* this product to make?

- How would your life be different if you weren't able to use X product?

- If you were CEO, how would you improve the website?

Incentives can increase your response rate

Aim for 200–400 responses in total. More is better, especially if you have multiple segments. Offering a small incentive increases the number of people willing to take part. This could be important if you have a small database or if your network is known to be unresponsive. A gift voucher is always popular but entry into a prize draw can also be used. Although purists say this affects the results, it is certainly preferable to having no data to work on.

Pitfalls to avoid

The primary goal of a survey is to learn about your customers but it should also yield insights that you can act on. Many of the surveys we come across are not actionable.

A common mistake is asking people to recall detail from memory. Take the question 'What almost stopped you buying from us?' It's a great question and one of our staples in the agency. However, it's more appropriate to ask immediately following a transaction, when details are still fresh in the memory.

Lastly, be careful how you report the results. Unless you have performed statistical analysis against a large enough sample, concrete conclusions are impossible. Statements like 'indications are...' and 'it appears that...' are perfectly fine. Just don't try and rely on these as the basis for business decisions as if they have statistical confidence.

Summary

Use a number of different data sources to get a full picture of your users, as well as the barriers and frustrations they experience on your site.

Take a balanced approach to research. Quantitative data tells you *what* is happening, whereas qualitative research can tell you *why* it is happening. Quantitative research and analysis can help you identify patterns whereas qualitative research is best used to discover new insights. At the same time, you should also aim for a mix of attitudinal and behavioural insights.

Personas and scenarios can help you to focus on what's important from a user's perspective. Every proposed intervention is aimed at changing the behaviour of your users and it is therefore vital that the entire process is centred on them. Though personas are fictional characters representing different user segments, they should be based on research, else they are pointless.

Create a segmented user journey map, using clickstream data. This gives you a good behavioural overview, shows where people are leaking out of your funnel and gives you an early steer on potential opportunities.

Usability testing is the process of observing your users interacting with your site or app. It is arguably the best method for uncovering usability issues. Automated user testing is easy to do but for more depth of understanding you should also try remote moderated user testing with people recruited live from your site.

E-mail surveys are a good way of getting to know your users and developing personas but not effective at examining usability problems. Include open-ended questions related to goals, attitude and motivation. Open text responses should be codified to facilitate quantitative analysis.

Notes

1 Reinhardt, A (1998) Steve Jobs: There's sanity returning, Business Week, 25 May 1998, http://www.bloomberg.com/news/articles/1998-05-25/steve-jobs-theres-sanity-returning (accessed: 1 July 2016).

2 Fried, J (2007) Ask 37signals: Personas?, 6 November 2007, https://signalvnoize.com/posts/690-ask-37signals-personas (accessed: 1 July 2016).

3 Long, F (2009) Real or Imaginary: The effectiveness of using personas in product design, *Irish Ergonomics Review*, Proceedings of the IES Conference 2009, Dublin, http://www.frontend.com/the-effectiveness-of-using-personas-in-product-design.html (accessed: 1 July 2016).

4 Cooper, A (2004) *The Inmates are Running the Asylum*, Sam's Publishing.

5 Bettencourt, L and Ulwick, A (2008) The customer-centered innovation map. https://hbr.org/2008/05/the-customer-centered-innovation-map/ar/1 (accessed: 1 July 2016).

6 Econsultancy (2015) Conversion Rate Optimization Report 2015 https://econsultancy.com/reports/conversion-rate-optimization-report/ (accessed: 1 July 2016).

7 Kaushik, A (2010) Web Analytics 2.0, Wiley, Indianapolis.

8 Nielsen, J (2014) Turn User Goals into Task Scenarios for Usability Testing, https://www.nngroup.com/articles/task-scenarios-usability-testing/ (accessed: 1 July 2016).

9 Nielsen, J & Landauer, T (1993) 'A mathematical model of the finding of usability problems,' Proceedings of ACM INTERCHI'93 Conference (Amsterdam, The Netherlands, 24–29 April 1993), pp 206–213.

Add depth
with further
research

05

Having dug the foundations, with additional research you can now build on that picture of your visitors and discover opportunities ripe for optimization. There is no particular sequence or priority for using these techniques and you might not even use all of them. What is important is to have a balance across the spectrum such as is depicted in Figure 4.1. Add new ones to fill in remaining gaps in your knowledge.

Heuristic evaluation

Many optimizers start the process with heuristic evaluation. However, it must be one of the most misunderstood concepts in CRO. If the evaluation is not carried out systematically, using a formal framework, it becomes diluted down to nothing more than one person's subjective opinion about the site.

The method was originally developed in 1990 by Dr Jakob Nielsen with Rolf Mollich, as a formal process of evaluating a website against ten general principles. It has subsequently been adapted for the purposes of CRO.

A framework for heuristic evaluation

These are the six principles we recommend you use for your heuristic evaluation:

1 Motivation
2 Value proposition
3 Relevance

4 Incentive and urgency

5 Distractions

6 Anxiety and friction

Motivation

Human behaviour and optimization are completely intertwined. The potential of any conversion is born out of a need. Underpinning that, a core motivation drives the customer through the decision-making process. The stronger the motivation, the more likely they are to purchase. Much of this happens at a visceral level, so understanding motivation comes from knowledge of the psychology behind it, as outlined in Chapter 3.

Value proposition

Strong motivation to purchase is not enough to clinch the sale, partly because the consumer has alternatives. They could buy from a competitor or choose to do nothing at all.

Your value proposition is central to persuading someone to take action. It is such an important concept that you'll find a separate section dedicated to it later in this chapter. For the purpose of the heuristic evaluation, you should be checking the following:

- Is the value proposition easy to understand?
- Is it communicated and articulated well?
- Is it credible?
- How does it stack up against the customer's expectations of value?
- Does it help customers imagine the difference the purchase will make in their lives?
- How does it compare against the value propositions of competitors?
- Is there a sense of uniqueness, of differentiation?

Relevance

Are the key messages relevant to the visitor, in the context of their motivation and need? Are they aligned with expectations that had been created upstream, for example in searching advertising campaigns? Is it specific and unambiguous? For example, if I clicked on an advert that promises 50 per cent discount, is that scent carried forward to the page that I arrive on? Do I see a reinforcing message with links to the marked down products? If not, there's a potential disruption of that initial thought pattern.

Incentive/urgency

Cialdini points out that, on the whole, people want to maximize gain and minimize cost (see Chapter 3). Is anything offered to sweeten the deal, or to make the user act now instead of delaying? Often, these mechanisms already exist but can be improved or amplified. For example, the incentive might be presented at the wrong time in the decision-making process. Or it might not be communicated compellingly enough.

Distractions

Humans have a limited attention span. Treat it as a scarce resource! Which elements on the page could be diverting attention from the main objectives? This can be fairly subtle. For example links in the main navigation, or other calls to action, can lead users down a side path further away from a sale.

Anxiety and friction

These are negative forces that get in the way of conversions, even when a user is highly motivated and everything else falls into place. Reducing anxiety and friction is therefore one of the easiest ways of improving the conversion rate.

The difference between the two is that anxiety plays out in the user's mind, whereas friction comes from the web page. Wondering whether fragile goods will arrive undamaged may cause anxiety. Being confronted by a long, badly designed form is an example of friction, as it increases the effort required on behalf of the user.

Do you see anything on the page that can potentially cause FUDs (Fear, Uncertainty, Doubt)? Is there any part of the process that could be simpler?

Setting up for heuristics evaluation

It's true that experienced optimizers can often spot great optimization opportunities just from looking at a site. But they almost certainly will not spot them all so you would be wise never to rely on the judgement of one individual, no matter how qualified and experienced that person may be.

The importance of having a diverse number of inputs was amply illustrated by an experiment conducted by Jakob Nielsen. He asked 19 evaluators to work together and they found 16 usability issues. No one picked up every issue and some evaluators spotted as few as three. The results are shown on

Figure 5.1 Jakob Nielsen's experiment. Black squares represent an opportunity spotted and white squares those that were missed

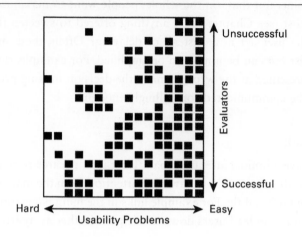

SOURCE Nielsen Norman Group (Nielsen, J (1995) Heuristic evaluation: How-to, Article by Jakob Nielsen. Available from: https://www.nngroup.com/articles/how-to-conduct-a-heuristic-evaluation/ (accessed: 1 July 2016)

the chart in Figure 5.1, with black squares representing an issue that was spotted and white those that were missed.

Look at the top row. You can see that the least successful evaluator only found three out of a possible 16 issues. On the far left of the chart, where the more hard-to-spot issues are plotted, there are only two black squares, indicating that that they were picked up by only two evaluators. Overall there are far more white squares than black, testament to just how difficult it can be. In fact, Nielsen also discovered that an evaluator typically finds only around a third of usability problems.

To get the best results with heuristic evaluation, follow these guidelines :

- **Use two or more people.** Different issues will be picked up by different individuals. Nielsen suggests using three to five.

- **Work collaboratively.** Although Nielsen recommends independent evaluations so that individuals aren't influenced by each other, our experience is that a collaborative effort works well. Having evaluators together in one session avoids duplication and saves time. Issues can be discussed and prioritized in real time, especially when there are opposing viewpoints. You don't even have to have everyone in one room. With video conferencing or screen-sharing, a group heuristic evaluation is just as effective when done remotely but always have one person keeping track of all the insights as they emerge.

- **Use a framework.** This allows you to systematically work through recognized heuristic principles which brings clarity and focus to the evaluation. Experienced optimizers should be given the freedom to walk through the site in search of opportunities, but even they are encouraged to apply a framework. Without that, it's simply an 'expert review', which generally only scratches the surface compared with a systematic heuristic evaluation.

To conduct a group heuristic evaluation, start by issuing a brief containing the following:

- **URL of the site,** or of specific pages if you're limiting it to an area of the site. If you're part of an organization, then presumably this is your own site. However, it doesn't have to be. It could form part of your competitor analysis, covered later in this chapter.
- **Framework** to be used. Have everyone use the same framework, or at least give everyone the same list of heuristics like the ones discussed above. Invite them to add on to the framework if they find something that's relevant but doesn't fit into one of the boxes.
- **Personas.** Even if you haven't yet fully developed all personas, some guidance is better than flying blind.
- **Scenarios,** shaped by the goals and needs of key personas.
- **Tasks** that the evaluator has to perform. These should flow from the scenarios. Keeping it somewhat vague will promote discovery and diversity of observations. So, rather than saying 'Type product X into the search box', you may want to go with 'Search for a product of your choice'.
- **Device.** Tell them which device to use.

You can collect responses either individually or in a group. If done individually, give everyone a template where they can list all the issues and opportunities they notice under relevant headings. Alternatively, ask them to use a screen capture tool, for example Jing, to take and annotate screen grabs with arrows pointing to the relevant areas. If evaluators collaborate, then have one person aggregate everything in real time.

You can also ask each evaluator to assign a score out of 10 to each heuristic and then plot it on a radar chart like the one below. In this example, the value proposition presents the biggest opportunity. This helps to quantify things but don't rely on this alone. The most valuable part of heuristic evaluation is the qualitative component where you describe issues and opportunities. Make that the focus.

Figure 5.2 Typical radar chart from an heuristic valuation, giving an overview of strengths and weaknesses

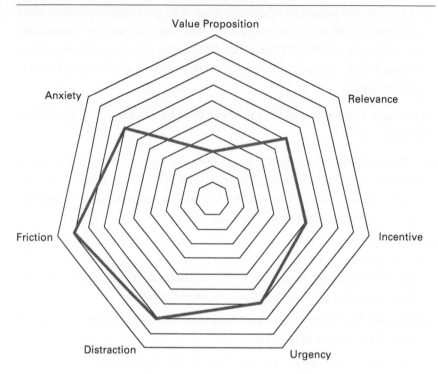

Interviews

Use interviews primarily to learn more about the motivations and attitudes of your users, and to build personas. Because of the relatively small sample size, you may sometimes want to conduct other forms of research to see if there is support for certain findings.

You can interview someone in person in their own environment, which has the advantage of giving you a first-hand feel for their context. However, it can be time consuming and expensive, and is not necessary in most cases. Telephone interviews have advantages of scale, efficiency and geographic reach.

As with surveys, the questions you ask should be guided by your objectives. The difference is that you can go into interviews with a few seed questions and allow the conversation to unfold naturally from there. Allow the interviewee to take you down unexpected paths. That's very much the point of an interview and a key advantage over surveys and even moderated usability testing. Most importantly, listen. Take notes obsessively. Repeat back what they have said to check you have understood their meaning but avoid putting words into their mouth. Let them do the talking: don't get in the way of that.

Customer interviews

'A deep dive into the lives of customers.'[1] That's how Steve Portigal, author of *Interviewing Users: How to Uncover Compelling Insights* describes it. Only by talking to customers can you truly begin to understand their context, needs, motivations and pain points. These are the things that fuel behaviour on your site. It is what your test hypotheses are built on. Don't skip it.

When I took over the operations of an online wine retailer, I dedicated part of one day each week to phoning a customer. I would steer the conversation around to the reasons why they bought from us. This was all about uncovering core motivation and understanding our value proposition from their perspective. At times, I would load a few cases in my car and do some deliveries myself, especially on weekends, when I knew people would be at home and in a position to talk. A few patterns quickly became apparent, for example how many orders were gifts. Well, it's wine. It figures. But we needed that personal interaction to have the confidence to develop a persona for the wine gifter. Without a doubt, this heightened understanding of the customer from informal ad hoc interviews helped to drive growth.

Interview customer service representatives

The operators in the incoming call centre, if you have one, have the thankless task of listening to people moan at them every day. What a gold mine! If you don't have a call centre, speak to your colleagues who deal with those customer calls.

Ask them to identify the three to five top queries and complaints. Explore the gamut of what goes wrong before an order is placed. What do website visitors ask about? And here is the secret sauce: also ask them how they respond.

They will know from experience how best to respond to the various customer queries. Tapping into that knowledge can inform a lot of test ideas. One of our clients makes a habit of spending a day in their call centre from time to time. She emerges full of ideas, focused on the customer's agenda.

Interview store managers and salespeople

If you operate in an omni-channel environment, do yourself a favour and spend time in your bricks and mortar stores. Shop assistants are at the sharp end of dealing with customers. They get real-time feedback and adjust their sales messages accordingly. They are in the incredibly privileged position of seeing how the purchase decision unfolds, hearing the burning questions and sales objections and learning which responses push undecided shoppers over the purchase line. Talk to them.

I recently visited a client's store to look at a high-ticket item that was a big seller, but had a high abandonment rate on their site. Seeing how the assistant 'sold' to me was an eye-opener, not only for me, but also for the client's online team when I later presented this to them. The pitch was completely different compared with the online approach. Why? Because that salesperson knew from talking to hundreds of customers how to pinpoint my needs and which buttons to push to help me make up my mind. Remember, your site is your online salesperson.

Most omni-channel stores will have Click and Collect counters. This is where your online customers interface with the business in the real world. What can the staff behind that counter share with you? What are their observations of your customers?

Feedback and transcript analysis

We've encouraged you to solicit user opinions and perspectives through surveys, but several feedback mechanisms are likely to be in place already. These include:

- Customer support e-mail address
- Live chat
- Social media
- Independent customer reviews

Analyse emails to the customer support address and live chat transcripts for common themes and patterns. Don't try to trawl through everything. Randomly select around 400 responses from each channel, going back every two to three months. Categorize the responses into headline topics so that you're able to identify and quantify the most important issues. Most live chat programs will show you on which pages queries originated, which adds another layer to this analysis.

Social media and customer reviews are visible to the world and may be a factor in the buying decision-making process. It's therefore good to know what is being said out there. How are customers alluding to the value proposition, in other words their net resulting experience of choosing your offer? What are the positive points that you could possible amplify? What are the negatives that you should maybe counter in the sales process? Are there product or other questions that can be incorporated into the copy on the site? What can you learn about the customers from their language?

Onsite polls

Shooting quick context-sensitive questions at your visitors while they're on your site can be a gold mine for getting to know them. But where it really comes into its own, is in situations where you want to examine certain onsite behaviour.

For example, a particular handbag Product Detail Page (PDP) on a client's site was able to draw in the crowds but there was then a battle to turn it into sales. Targeting only those visitors who looked like they were leaving the site from this page, we asked bluntly: 'Why did you not purchase this handbag?' A few comments suggested that they were not sure what to match the handbag with. It was an insight that we could act on and not even close to what we had anticipated.

Lock onto the problem by targeting your questions as precisely as possible. Is a particular product category performing below average? Ask users on those pages what's missing or why they won't buy. High basket abandonment rate? Ask abandoners why they're leaving. Mobile site not converting? Target mobile visitors to understand them better. Are there potential anxieties or friction (see heuristic evaluation above) that you want to explore? Invite users on that page to tell you about it.

Figure 5.3   An example of a Qualaroo onsite poll box

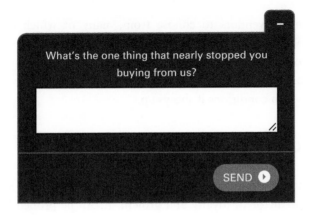

SOURCE Image courtesy of Qualaroo

In our experience, most users respond favourably to one or two well-placed polls as it gives them an opportunity to raise any feedback they may have. But it can be annoying if done too aggressively. Use it sparingly to fill specific gaps in your knowledge of customers and their behaviour. Limit the number of surveys and questions that a user will see.

As before, the questions you ask depend on your situation and objectives. Identify the gaps in your knowledge before popping the question. Popular examples are:

Landing pages and intent

- What is the purpose of your visit today?
- What were you expecting to find on this page?
- What persuaded you to visit our site rather than that of a competitor?

Abandonment/hesitation

- If you didn't make a purchase, please tell us why not?
- What could have persuaded you to check out?
- What is holding you back from making a purchase?

Post-purchase exit

- What was the one thing that almost stopped you buying from us?
- How did you justify the investment in this product?
- What was your biggest fear or concern about buying from us?
- Which other options did you consider before choosing this product?
- What persuaded you to buy X product instead of Y?

There are many vendors to choose from, many of which are listed in Chapter 2. We use Qualaroo almost routinely (Figure 5.3). It slides a little question box in from the bottom of the page, where it sits until it's interacted with or dismissed. You can configure its appearance, as well as where and under which conditions it shows up.

Satisfaction survey

According to Harvard Business Review,[2] the Net Promoter Score (NPS) is the best predictor of loyalty and growth. It can be probed by email or via an onsite poll. If done online, you can decide to target customers only by posting it on the purchase confirmation page, or cast the net wider by having it earlier in the funnel. The main question is:

- How likely are you to recommend our company to a friend or colleague?

Users are asked to choose a response on a scale from 0 to 10. To calculate your NPS, subtract the number of detractors (0 – 6) from promoters (9 and 10). Tools like Qualaroo handle this automatically.

To make it more actionable, ask a follow-up question:

- What is the reason for your response?

Using pivot tables in Excel, you can easily map these reasons to the numerical rating the respondent provided. Look carefully at the issues raised by detractors. They are shouting: 'Fix me or your business will die.' Some will be outside your sphere of influence – escalate them to the relevant managers. Write down the ones that can be treated with split tests, and then keep any eye out for further confirmation on them from other data sources.

Customer immersion

One of the most revealing ways to find out what it's really like to buy from your site is to become a customer yourself. You may be astonished at what you discover.

The exercise is often done as an extension of heuristic evaluation. Place an order, just as if you were a customer; the only difference is you log each step and take notice of your actions, feelings and observations. Your aim is to inspect the entire purchase chain, including the checkout process as well as the post-purchase experience. Since the devil is often in the detail, venture into all those nooks and crannies where your visitors end up. For example, you could check the password reset procedure. Screenshot the process, look at the emails sent to you after requesting a new password and see if there are gaps.

Often, the last mile is owned by a courier service. For a pure play e-commerce business, that may be the only human interface with the customer. Many people won't make a distinction between your business and the carrier, so what impression is left? Try to return the item. How easy or cumbersome is that? Compare the reality you experience to the messaging and promises on the site. Does it match up? Is there something in the experience you can improve? Are there positive elements around the fulfilment currently not reflected online? For example, one of our clients had a white glove delivery service that we discovered by chance after placing an order. It was actually a pleasant delivery experience – but not a word of it in key places on the site!

Competitor analysis

Don't confuse this with copying competitors, which is unfortunately all too common. That's not wise, because as CRO thought leader Peep Laja said, 'They don't know what they're doing either.'[3] The purpose is to see your offer from your customer's perspective since their expectations may be shaped by the messages of competitors.

- Do a Google search for your offer, using different phrases. For ideas on what to search by, look at the area in Google Analytics that shows you phrases used by your visitors before arriving at your site.

- Which competing offers come up in the results? What is their core message? What value claims do they make, both in organic and paid search results?

- Visit the competitor sites and their social media accounts, and take note of their key messages and value claims. How compelling is their offer compared with yours? Also review competitors that respondents may have flagged that have not come up in the search results.

Classify and document your competitors' core messages, benefits and value claims to create a table similar to the one below. The idea is to be aware of the messages that your users are exposed to.

This table gives you a quick overview of the messages that your target market is most exposed to. That's not to say that the same things are what matters to your customers. How does it compare with what they told you in surveys? Is there anything your users rated that is drowned in white noise? Is there any space in the landscape of messages that you can own?

You could also use information-gathering tools like iSpionage to investigate your competitors' advertising campaigns, which can add interesting context.

Table 5.1 Summary table of analysis of your competitors' core messages

Core themes	Competitors									Total
	1	2	3	4	5	6	7	8	9	
Price guarantee		✔						✔		2
Free shipping		✔	✔	✔	✔	✔	✔		✔		7
Locally made	✔									1

Value proposition

A whole plethora of research points to a link between a well-developed value proposition and business success.[4] Without a compelling value proposition, your visitor may not convert, even if they came to your site with the strong intention of buying. As such, value proposition is a central tenet of many CRO models. MECLABS deems it to be 'a major key to conversions',[5] while WiderFunnel goes further: 'Your value proposition determines your potential conversion rate.'[6]

Unfortunately, the true ethos of the concept has been diluted over the years. It's often confused with the USP (Unique Selling Proposition), but it's not the same thing.[7] Neither is it those boxes dotted around the site, shouting 'Free delivery' and 'Money Back Guarantee.' That's not the only misrepresentation of the concept. Michael Lanning, the McKinsey consultant who first coined the term, laments:

'Often, the term 'value proposition' has been misinterpreted as the simplistic marketing notion of positioning, the meagre content of which is largely antithetical to the term's true meaning.'[8]

So then, what is the value proposition?

It boils down to this question:

'Why should I buy from you as opposed to your competitor?'

Answered from a customer perspective – not yours, it captures the essence of your value proposition. But there's more to it.

Fundamentally, it's a promise of value to your customers, as the name suggests. The customer's perception of it, that is, not yours. Value is commonly defined as:

$$Value = Benefits - Cost$$

Key here is to figure out how to tip this value equation in your favour. The more you can increase perceived benefits, and decrease perceived cost, the more likely a sufficiently motivated visitor is to purchase. Reducing price is not usually a wise business move, so you should:

- add benefits, or at least amplify perceived benefits in your messaging
- make sure these benefits resonate with your customers
- reduce perceived cost, which is not the same as lowering price.

It's easy to go into product-centric tunnel-vision mode, which you should resist. This is because benefits relate mainly to products, whereas the value proposition encompasses the *total experience* of the customer. Lanning defines the value proposition as 'the entire set of resulting experiences' that your customer has by buying from you.

As an example, here's a story from when I was running an online store. Earlier, I mentioned how I sometimes did deliveries so that I could meet customers. A slightly annoyed lady pondered loudly why her husband kept buying 'all this wine', when there was nowhere to put any more boxes.

Thinking of the value equation above, the perceived cost for the customer (the wine-buying husband) includes the price of the item itself (an expensive premium wine), storage challenges and justifying the purchase to his wife.

That's quite a lot of costs, yet overall there must have been sufficient benefits for it to have value, because he bought and paid good money for it.

When I spoke to him later, I realized that it was not the *wine* he was buying. He was buying the net resulting *experience*. Despite the price tag, storage problems and nagging wife, he was still one up. How?

Only a few cases of this rare wine were available, so firstly there was the badge of owning something quite exclusive. What really sealed the deal though, was the prospect of sharing it with his dinner guests. Who wouldn't feel special? Who wouldn't be impressed with our customer's taste for the finer things in life? So who are the lucky dinner guests, I asked. Astoundingly, there was no confirmed dinner date. Such is the power of the total net experience, that an imagined event sold an expensive case of wine, which ended up being squeezed into a cupboard.

Discover your value proposition

Discover is a deliberate choice of word. Business often talks about *determining* the value proposition, but that's the wrong mindset. Your value promise will not matter to customers unless it matches *their* perception of value. Management is unfortunately often out of sync with the reality of their customers. In a study of 326 firms by management consultants Bain & Co, 80 per cent believed they were providing a superior customer experience. However, only 8 per cent of their customers thought that was the case![9]

Ask your customers what matters to them. Here are some questions that can give you this insight:

- What made you buy from us as opposed to a competitor?
- What made you buy from a competitor instead of us?
- What persuaded you to make this purchase?

- How did you justify the expense?
- How will product X make your life better?
- How would things be different if you stopped using product X?

Another way to determine what matters to your customers is to analyse search marketing performance. Compare the Click Through Rates (CTR) of Pay Per Click (PPC) advertisements, including paused campaigns. Divide everything into broad themes based on the propositions in the headlines and ad content. A typical e-commerce site may end up with categories like price match, free delivery, range, guarantee, etc. Are there any patterns when you compare the CTR performance across these broad categories? You may find that your users consistently respond more favourably to one theme over another. That could be a signal to incorporate this theme in your value proposition.

Incidentally, it's also possible to test candidate value propositions by using the same method. You have the benefit of far more traffic in search results than you have on your site, and it's a relatively inexpensive way of validating your value proposition. Create different text advertisements, each containing a distinct value theme. Then, compare the results over a period of time in the same way as explained above.

Crafting a value proposition

When creating your value proposition, consider the following:

- What are the things that customers tell you matter most to them when they consider buying from you?
- How does the customer think choosing your offer would improve their life? Whether it really transpires is irrelevant. What is important is their impression when making the buying decision.
- What promises of value are offered by your competitors? To what extent do they match the desires of your customers? What gaps does this leave for you? Refer to the section on competitive analysis earlier in this chapter.

How to communicate the value proposition

Lanning offers three characteristics of a well-communicated value proposition:[10]

Clarity

Make it easy for the customer to visualize the net resulting experience. For example, images and sensory language can help us to feel and taste something. It can help us to experience the product in our mind, the power of which should not be underestimated.

Differentiation

What is unique about your offer? What makes it stand out from the alternatives? Remember, for your customer doing nothing is also an option.[11] This is key to creating a superior net resulting experience that overcomes both competitors and consumer inertia.

Credibility

People are sceptical about marketing messages and 'sales talk'. Your statement needs to have 'verisimilitude' or the appearance of truth. Below are a few things you can do to improve the credibility of your claims. You'll see some of it put into practice in Figure 5.4:

- Offer objective support, such as ratings, testimonials and endorsements.
- Be specific. For example, '2,378 products in stock' sounds more credible than 'we have the largest range'.
- Use language that resonates with your customers. To achieve this, many copywriters draw inspiration from qualitative customer surveys. They may even quote specific phrases used by customers.
- Connect with a persona. Create your value messages for that one person.

Value proposition case study

This case study shows a compelling value proposition, forcefully communicated on an e-commerce site, the UK's largest retailer of specialist toys and food for exotic birds.

Heather is a widow in her late 60s, living in the north of England. Her parrot is more than a pet, he's a companion, a child ('perpetual toddler' in her words). She is the persona around whom this page was developed.

You'll never hear Heather refer to 'my parrot' – only by his name, Buddy. She loves buying nice things for him, but is always concerned about his safety, as toys that come apart from rough parrot play can cause injury. She heard about Northern Parrots from another parrot owner, whose vet had recommended them.

Figure 5.4 This value-infused homepage delivered a sizeable uplift in Revenue Per Visitor (RPV) as it matched the desires of key personas

Everything your Parrot needs - delivered next day

Find something for your Parrot

African Grey (843)

What are you looking for?

- Food (181)
- Toys (456)
- Cages (26)
- Accessories (145)
- Supplements (46)

Click to find

Choose from the UK's widest range of Parrot supplies

With over 1,500 toys, foods, cages and accessories for Parrots and cockatiels, budgies, lovebirds and more, we're the UK's favourite Parrot supplies store.

You won't find a bigger range anywhere else. In fact, we have so many high quality products that many pet shops and online stores buy from us and vets regularly recommend us.

Plus, you're guaranteed a fantastic service with 97.1% of UK orders delivered in 2 days or less. We've delivered abroad to 123 countries, and since we started in 1995 have made more than 250,000 birds very happy.

"I regularly refer my clients to Northern Parrots as I know they can get whatever they need for their Parrot quickly and reliably"

Richard Jones (BVSc MSc MRCVS)
Avian Veterinarian
Northwich, Cheshire

SOURCE Image courtesy of Northern Parrots, www.northernparrots.com

We knew what customers valued from surveys and interviews. We changed the homepage, Heather's entry point, replacing the hero image at the top of the page with messaging that reflected those insights:

- Trusted shop, recommended by veterinarians – so your parrot is safe
- Widest range of things for your parrot – so your parrot can have fun, playing with something new
- Next day delivery – so your parrot doesn't have to wait

This home page also included a subtle re-write of the client's previous headline from 'Everything you need for your parrot' to 'Everything your parrot needs'. This may only be a few words of difference but the former is a promise to Heather, while the latter is a promise to the parrot and it is the parrot's needs that are really important to Heather.

Visitor behaviour maps

There are many different types of visitor behaviour maps. These are visual representations of user activity. It's especially effective in presentations to and discussions with stakeholders, to create talking points around user behaviour. Largely based on mouse movements, they show you how people interact with your pages. Most common are:

- Heatmaps
- Clickmaps
- Scroll maps
- Mouse movement maps
- Confetti maps
- Overlay maps
- List views
- Attention maps
- Gaze plot maps

There are two main types of heatmap software. The first is clickmap software, which creates visual heatmaps based on real user behaviour tracked on your website. It runs on your site and monitors the mouse movement and click patterns of visitors. Reports are based on actual data.

Table 5.2 A breakdown of the different types of visitor behaviour visualization tools

Type of heatmap	What it shows	Use the data to...
Scrollmap	How far down your page your visitors are scrolling	Identify whether the content you want your visitors to see is being noticed or whether you need to re-organize the page to put the most important content in a more prominent location on the page
Mouse movement map	Where your visitors are moving their mouse to and what elements they're hovering over	Infer where your website visitors are looking based on their mouse movements. Identify links with a low mouse movement-to-click ratio, which implies that users look at it, but choose not to interact
Clickmap	Where your website visitors are clicking on your web page	Discover where visitors click, and importantly, where they don't click. Are they clicking on elements that are not linked?
Overlay map	Click activity for each item on the page	Get exact numbers of clicks on each link, rather than comparing shades of colours
Confetti map	A segmented view of where your website visitors are clicking	Analyse clicks by visitor type. For example, how does the behaviour of PPC, e-mail and organic traffic differ? Do visitors who convert behave any differently than those who don't convert?
List view	Quantifies clicks on visible and non-visible areas of your web page	Compare the user engagement with every element of your web page. Which items on the drop down navigation are most popular? Which are the most popular products in your carousel?
Attention map	Algorithmic prediction of which areas on the page attract the most attention, before a visitor clicks	Discover whether content you want your visitors to see and read is visible enough. Are visitors likely to notice your value proposition? Are there distractions?
Gaze plot	Where your visitors are looking, in what order they look at on-page items and how long they look at them for	Understand how your visitors are viewing your web page – what is drawing their attention? How long are they looking at or reading your copy? Where do people look after they've looked at the product?

Related to this is predictive software which reflects on the ability of a design to distribute attention effectively. These scan an image, like your live web page or a wireframe, and use algorithms and artificial intelligence to show which parts are most likely to catch the attention of a viewer. It is a predictive model, developed by analysing thousands of eye tracking movements, and powered by algorithms and artificial intelligence to replicate the real thing with high accuracy.

Heatmaps show you exactly where people clicked on a page, regardless of whether it's a link or not. The more clicks, the brighter the spot. It shows which elements on a page generate the most interest. Look at it critically. Does it make sense, or are there surprises? Are people clicking where you want them to click? Are they being distracted or going down less profitable paths? Is it because of design, or does it possibly tell you something about your visitors' goals, needs and intentions? What can you infer about user behaviour by looking at the distribution of clicks?

As with most analysis, the most interesting jewels of insight are usually hidden in segmentation. Don't ever miss this trick. You may find, for example, that mobile users behave very differently compared with other device types. In the clickmap of the login page in Figure 5.5, new visitors are represented by grey dots and returning visitors are light dots. A large number of new visitors appear to be interacting with the login area. This prompts the question – why? Surely, if they were new to the site, they would not previously have registered an account to log into. This insight may lead to the hypothesis that the distinction is not clear enough and should be better messaged.

The idea behind scrollmaps is to show you how far down the page visitors scroll, and specifically how much of what happens 'below the fold' is noticed. The fold is a concept inherited from newspapers, which are of course literally folded in half on the newsstand. Passers-by can only see the top half of the page, which is meant to grab the attention. In a similar way, only the top section of your web page is visible when a user first looks at it. Does it work hard enough in generating interest? What percentage of people see key content if it's further down the page? Are there any areas lower down that receive a lot of attention? Why would that be and should you elevate that content?

If possible, integrate the heat- and scrollmap tool with your split testing platform so that you can compare performance of test variations against the control (original) and make inferences about how your variation changes behaviour. Some split testing platforms, like Visual Website

Figure 5.5 Segmented clickmap of a login page, where grey dots are new visitors and light dots are returning visitors

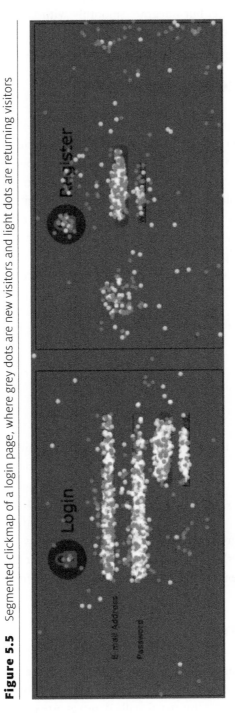

SOURCE Image courtesy of Crazy Egg

Optimizer (VWO), have built-in heatmapping capabilities. Others may not offer this feature, but integrate smoothly with Crazy Egg or another heatmapping service.

Session recordings

Rather than static images, these tools show you videos of mouse movements and clicks of users interacting with your site. Watching these clips can be revealing, but it can also be a laborious and time-consuming task if not managed properly. Each video covers one user session, and it can add up quickly. Avoid aimlessly replaying everything from beginning to end.

In the discovery phase, look at a couple of clips in each area of the site just to get an overview. There's a lot to be learnt about visitor behaviour in this way. It can help you identify usability issues, errors and sources of friction and anxiety. Cover the main points of user interaction such as:

- navigation
- call to action buttons
- product images
- reviews
- forms
- search

However, the tool is best used to illuminate specific questions, or to investigate a particular issue. To do this, you can filter clips based on pages visited, device type and other conditions. Pick your area of interest and watch just those videos back to back at high speed. For example, you could watch only people who abandoned straight after site search. Or examine the progression from Product Listing Pages (PLPs) to Product Detail Pages (PDPs). Shoot for 100–200 recordings per key area of the site. Slice it into different device categories to compare performance on mobile.

Onsite search

It's amazing how much you can tell about user intent and needs by analysing the phrases used to search your site. Site searchers also tend to be more prolific spenders so this journey usually deserves attention. You simply need to set up Google Analytics (GA) to start tracking this data.

Table 5.3 Data obtained from GA that compares the behaviour of visitors who used site search versus those who didn't

Site search status	Sessions	Revenue contribu- tion	Average order value	E-commerce conversion rate	Per session value
Without Site Search	86%	60%	£17.87	4.40%	£0.79
With Site Search	14%	40%	£30.92	10.25%	£3.17

Start by comparing the behaviour of searchers against non-searchers. Table 5.3 shows, an actual example. What's so revealing is that only a very small percentage of visitors use site search – about 14 per cent – but they're responsible for a massive 40 per cent of revenue.

Conversion rate and Average Order Value are more than double. Even a small improvement in this funnel could yield big results. This is quite a common observation and it's easy to hypothesize that pushing more visitors into the search funnel will make you rich. It's not that simple. Site searchers may already be more motivated to purchase.

It's usually better to look for ways to optimize the search experience. That starts with understanding the current search journey. To get an overview, start by looking at the following:

- Most common search terms
- Terms with highest/lowest exit rates
- Terms with highest/lowest conversion rates
- Top search terms ranked by Revenue/Per Search Value
- Pages where most search events originate
- Failed search terms

Review your search results pages for the 20 most searched terms. Often, just improving the performance of the Top 20 can have an impact. Are the most relevant products displayed first? There's some research that suggests that users pay disproportionately more attention to the first few items. Are there any distractions? Too much choice perhaps?

Take a step back from the search pages and look at your site with a fresh eye in light of what you know people are searching for. Are the products that people search for prominently displayed on your homepage, category pages and other relevant areas? If not, then putting them in sight could boost sales.

The GA metric *per cent Search Exits* tells you the percentage of people who left your site straight after doing a search. Sort this by column to see which search terms are causing most dropouts. Now run a search for those terms with high exit rates to see if you can figure out why they're causing visitors to give up. Are the search results relevant? Are they presented in a way that can cause confusion, friction or distraction? Conduct a similar search on your main competitor's site. How do you compare? The purpose is to look at it in the same context as your visitor, never to copy what competitors are doing.

You can also see how demand is influenced by seasonality, such as the time of year. To find out, export the top unique searches for each month over the last year from GA. Then stitch them together in 12 columns, one for each month. Are there patterns that you can pick up? How does that inform merchandising decisions? Does it potentially have any impact on your Optimization Plan? Could you use this data to inform your promotional plans?

With a little extra configuration, you can track failed searches in GA. This will show you which search queries return no results. Are products not showing because they're not in stock or has something else gone wrong? If you don't carry the products that users are searching for, is that an opportunity? What has brought your visitors under the impression that they can buy something from you that you don't stock?

Looking at the pages your users were on when they started their search will give you different insights. Are there any surprises when you look at this report? For example, what does it mean if a lot of people search for things from the product detail pages? Are they not finding what they were looking for? How do search patterns differ between page templates? For example, do people in the checkout funnel search for delivery information?

Do buyers search for the same things as non-buyers? Do people from a certain location express different needs in their search activity? As with any GA report, depth of insight improves with segmentation. At the very least you want to compare search patterns across device categories, but think about what other segments may be relevant for your business.

Form analysis

How much do you like filling in forms? Nobody does and yet forms are central in many online journeys. It's easy to see how they can get in the way of conversions. To illustrate this, an analysis of data from 650,000 form users revealed that the conversion rate for Order/Payment forms averaged only 9 per cent![12]

Assess the performance of pages containing forms in GA. First, review top level indicators for those pages such as bounce rate, exit rate and drop-off rate. This will give you some context and direction in terms of which forms to analyse and prioritize. As for the forms, essentially you want to be able to answer the following questions:

- How many people saw the form?
- How many started filling it out?
- How many completed the form?
- Which fields caused users to abandon?

The good news is that all of this data can be made available to you by setting up event tracking in GA, which involves just a tiny bit of technical work for your developer.

Another approach may be to use a tool designed for this purpose. They can show you things such as which fields cause the most hesitation, where errors occur and can identify the fields that lead to abandonment. If forms are central in your visitor journey, or if you have problematic forms, it may be worth investing in bespoke software like Formisimo. Hotjar, Inspectlet and Clicktale also offer form analytics packages.

Session recordings, discussed in detail earlier, can also come in handy. Filter recordings of people interacting with the form in question. You should spot the issues as you review the clips: where people pause, errors that come up, and where they abandon.

Finally, you may find it helpful to conduct a heuristic evaluation, focused specifically on forms. Here are some widely recognized principles, which you could use as a basis for the evaluation and, later on, test hypotheses:

- **Form length**. The more fields, the more daunting the task will appear. Every field has to justify its existence. Do you really need a name? And surname? Why do you need it? Could e-mail address suffice? Another way of reducing form length is to use progressive disclosure. This lets users see only what's relevant and then the form dynamically builds itself to reveal new fields based on the user's input.
- **Progress bar:** will your users be less likely to give up if they know where they are in the form and how much longer they have to go?
- **Layout:** would a single column form with the field name above be better than two columns with the field name to the side?

- **Nomenclature:** what you call a part of the form can make a difference to how people react. For example, 'verification required' may be off-putting, whereas 'activate now' sounds perhaps more inviting.

- **Phone number:** people generally resist sharing their phone number. If you need it, could you tell the user why it's in their interest to provide it? For example 'We may call you to schedule delivery.'

- **Password:** imagine you're gliding through all these easy questions like name and e-mail, when suddenly you're forced to provide a password. Should it be the same as the one you use for Facebook? Oh no, turns out that doesn't meet the password requirements for this site. Why didn't they signpost how many characters, capitals and symbols you need, before you fill it in. Next, you have to enter it twice – why?! Don't they trust you that you'll get it right? You can see how quickly this becomes a source of friction.

- **CAPTCHA:** do you really need it? If so, make it as easy as possible. A simple puzzle like 3+1= means they only have to type in one digit, not a string that you struggle to read. Or just a tick box to indicate they're not a robot?

- **Error messages:** is the error message specific to the error? Does it leave the user with instructions on how to correct it? Does the message make it sound as though the user is at fault? Is it worded in a helpful way so the user understands what to do? Is it in close proximity to where the error occurred?

Exclusion split tests

Split testing is discussed in detail in later chapters, because it comes later in the optimization process. However, there is one type of split test that you can actually build into the insights generation phase.

Exclusion split tests involve creating a new variation of a page with one element hidden, such as removing the words 'Free delivery when you spend £X or more'. From this, you can discover how important this element is to your visitors and whether it has a material influence on sales.

What you can learn from exclusion split tests

What makes them so great is that you're not relying on what people tell you but on what they do. You're seeing it for yourself. Running this sort of test this early on in the process gives you valuable insight into the various conversion levers on your site.

In the 'Free Delivery' example from earlier, you could try testing the same message higher up the funnel (ie on the home and category pages) or further down the funnel (ie within the basket and checkout pages) and see if you get a different result. All of these insights collectively can further your understanding of the customer decision-making process throughout their journey on your site.

Like all split tests, when you run an exclusion split test, there are three possible outcomes: your variation could be better, worse or the same as the original in terms of Revenue Per Visitor or some other KPI. What does this tell you?

If it's better: removing the element increases the KPI.

Do you really need that element? Does it fulfil a business need – in which case can you develop a hypothesis around testing alternative executions or positions – or can it be removed?

Why does something that on the surface should improve sales, actually hinder them? What can you learn about your visitors' wants, needs and motivations? This could be fruitful ground for more exploration.

If it's worse: removing the element reduces the KPI.

You have confirmation that this particular element features strongly in the decision-making process.

What other insight can you draw from it? Can you amplify this message, or principle, either on this page or elsewhere in the funnel? Should you test alternative messages or design executions of this element?

If it's inconclusive: removing the element has no impact on the KPI.

This suggests that this element in its current form neither helps nor hinders target behaviour on this page. Do you really need that element? Could you downgrade its importance, in order to allow you to give other elements increased visibility in the eye path?

Also think about the wider impact. What does it mean that a given element doesn't influence behaviour strongly? Could you run exclusion tests of the same element elsewhere in the funnel?

Technical site performance audit

So far we've emphasized learning about site visitors and customers. It's also worth examining the performance of the site itself in the following areas, which can all impact on the ability to generate revenue. Any insights generated from this analysis will become JDI (Just Do It) recommendations, rather than split tests. Send the findings and any suggested fixes straight to your development team.

Site speed

The *Average Page Load Time* report in GA shows how quickly each individual page loaded compared to the site average. Note down the worst performing pages. Segment this report by device category, browser and even country if relevant to your business. Google also offers advice on how to fix that.

To find out how long each page takes to load and identify bottlenecks, use some software such as Pingdom (free version available at tools.pingdom.com). This breaks down the page into file requests, showing the time it takes for each one to load and exactly where bottlenecks occur. It also gives suggestions for fixes.

YSlow is a browser extension that grades the page based on a list of performance rules. Visit those pages identified by GA as being the worst offenders. Copy the suggested fixes to send to your developers.

Cross-browser and cross-device testing

The Browser & OS report in GA will show you the conversion rate broken down by browser, and will help you to identify ones that perform below average. For the most accurate results, look at one device category at a time by applying an advanced filter for desktop, tablet or mobile. Check in the 'Sessions' column that a given browser makes up enough of the total audience to be taken notice of. Get an overview of the mobile devices used by your visitors in the Devices report.

Load your site in the devices and browsers identified in the above exercise. If you don't have access to those, use any of the cloud-based emulators listed below. Walk through your site, using a typical user flow, touching all the important sections eg homepage, site search, PLP, PDP, Add to Cart, Basket, Checkout etc.

- browserstack.com
- crossbrowsertesting.com
- deviceanywhere.com
- appthwack.com

Summary

Research and analysis is the foundation of effective website optimization. Start off with personas and journey mapping and then add colour with techniques discussed in this chapter.

Heuristic evaluation is the process of evaluating a site against a predetermined set of principles. The heuristics most commonly found in CRO models are motivation, value proposition, relevance, incentives, distractions, friction and anxiety.

Your value proposition can be summarized as the answer to this question: 'Why should I buy from you as opposed to your competitor?' This should go beyond features and benefits to encompass the entire experience.

The value proposition will have to compete with claims made by competitors so conduct a competitive analysis to be aware of that context. Audit core themes that your users are exposed to and make a judgement on how you fit in with that.

Surveys and onsite polls are a cost-effective way of getting into the mind of your user and to fill specific gaps in your knowledge. Feedback channels, such as live chat and customer support e-mails can add different layers of insight.

Behaviour visualization such as heatmaps, scrollmaps, click maps and session recordings can show you how people navigate, where they clicked and how far they scroll down the page. Site search analysis can reveal user intent and seasonal trends.

Exclusion split tests are designed to quantify the value of elements that exist on the site. By hiding an element in a variation, you will get unique insight into what matters to your customers, and it could prepare the ground for later split tests.

Don't forget to do a comprehensive technical audit. This should include page load checks, as well as cross-browser and device performance. Often, this is where you find the easy pickings.

Notes

1 Portigal, Steve (2013) Interviewing Users: How to Uncover Compelling Insights, Rosenfeld Media.

2 Reichheld, Frederick (2003) The One Number You Need to Grow, Harvard Business Review, available from: https://hbr.org/2003/12/the-one-number-you-need-to-grow (accessed: 1 July 2016)

3 Laja, P (2013) Stop copying your competitors: They don't know what they're doing either, available from: http://conversionxl.com/stop-copying-your-competitors-they-dont-know-what-theyre-doing-either/ (accessed: 1July 2016)

4 John A. Parnell (2006) Generic strategies after two decades: a reconceptualization of competitive strategy, Management Decision, 44 (8), pp 1139–1154; Lusch, R, Vargo, S & Tanniru, M (2010) 'Service, value networks and learning', Journal of the Academy of Marketing Science, 38, pp 19–31

5 Jacobson, A (2008) Powerful Value Propositions, available from: http://www.marketingexperiments.com/improving-website-conversion/powerful-value-propositions.html (accessed: 1 July 2016)

6 Goward, C (2013) Use these 3 points to create an awesome value proposition, available from: http://www.widerfunnel.com/conversion-rate-optimization/how-to-create-an-awesome-value-proposition (accessed: 1 July 2016)

7 Lanning, Michael J (2015) MJL MECLs Intrv Total [online video] available from: https://www.youtube.com/watch?v=-Bzqlxnh9uw&feature=youtu.be (accessed: 1 July 16)

8 Lanning, M (2000) Delivering profitable value: A revolutionary framework to accelerate growth, generate wealth and rediscover the heart of business, p 61, Perseus Books, New York

9 Allen, J, Reichheld, F, Hamilton, B and Markey, R (2005) Closing the delivery gap, available at: http://www.bain.com/bainweb/pdfs/cms/hotTopics/closingdeliverygap.pdf (accessed: 1 July 2016)

10 Helmut, M and Lanning, M (2016) Communicating the value proposition: how to turn a brilliant product idea into a marketing success, available at: http://www.dpvgroup.com/articleswhite-papersbook/articles-white-papers/communicating-the-value-proposition/ (accessed: 1 July 2016)

11 Anderson, J and Narus, J (1998) Business marketing: Understand what customers value, *Harvard Business Review*, 76 (6), pp 53–65

12 Formstack (2015), The 2015 Form Conversion Report, available from: https://www.formstack.com/infographics/form-conversion-report-2015 (accessed: 1 July 2016)

Merchandising analytics 06

'A website converts because customers want to buy the merchandise presented to them,' said Kevin Hillstrom, one of the world's experts in data mining.[1] It therefore follows that to optimize your website and sell more you need to show your visitors things they want to buy. But how do you know?

The answer lies in a specialist form of research and analysis known as Merchandising Analytics. It involves looking in detail at the interaction between your customers and the product ranges, including categories and pricing.

There are several different Merchandising Analytics techniques you can use to find out where within your existing product range you can squeeze more sales. Two methods recommended by Hillstrom stand out:

- **New Product Analysis** – the rate at which new products are introduced and their productivity (ie: contribution of each new product to total sales)
- **Bestsellers Analysis** – the rate of decay of best-selling items

Other valuable techniques include:

- Product category analysis
- Look-to-book analysis
- Price point analysis
- Price testing

New product analysis

Hillstrom advocates that businesses need to constantly introduce new products and cultivate them to bestseller status in order to be truly successful.[2] Merchandising Analytics is a brilliant way to help you achieve this. Here's how you do it.

Introducing new products

The first step is to analyse what you're doing now. Total up the quantity of new items introduced over the previous three years and the revenue they have generated. If a product was introduced in year one then you will need to capture the revenue it took in its first year and years two and three.

If a product was introduced in year two or three, you will need to pro-rata them to calculate their likely sales over this three-year period. For example, if you had first year sales of £100,000, multiply this by three to get the total sales over a three-year period. It's a little rough and ready but will suffice for your analysis.

You will end up with a table that looks something like Table 6.1.

This simple exercise can be quite an eye-opener. For example, in the scenario above, we can see that over the last three years:

- The rate at which new products have been introduced has fallen by 25 per cent from 393 per year to 391 per year.

- Sales from new products have plummeted by 41 per cent from £3.5 million to just over £2 million.

- Productivity – the total sales that each new product contributes – has also gone down, by 22 per cent from around £9k to around £7k.

This fictional example paints a gloomy picture. New products are the life-blood of many e-commerce websites and here it's ebbing away. 'Businesses that develop new merchandise today will experience marketing success tomorrow,' according to Hillstrom, so the declining sales and productivity from new products could have a detrimental effect on the business's ability to attract new customers and retain existing ones.

Table 6.1 Example showing total new product revenue and average revenue per new product over last three years

Year	Number of new products introduced	Revenue from new products	Productivity of new products
1	383	£3,546,011	£9,258
2	320	£2,889,318	£9,029
3	291	£2,111,065	£7,254

How to identify potential new products

Continuing with the above example, this picture may lead the company to launch more new products. So, what products should they introduce? Simply putting a bigger range of a number of new products does not guarantee high sales. Not all new products are a success, so revenue from the shiny new items may not make up for all that has been lost.

How can you improve the chances of introducing high-performing new products rather than duds? If you're looking for rich sources of inspiration for successful new product development try the following:

- Look at your onsite failed search, where visitors typed in something they were looking for but it came up with no matches. This is a golden insight into what people really want to buy from you.

- Rank your products by sales then look at the bestsellers to identify common themes.

- Use search data to analyse trends and search terms that correspond to your current categories and products, for example if you sell mirrors, look at volume of searches for 'oval mirrors', 'round mirrors', etc.

- Identify categories that are growing in sales and items that are doing better than expected. Develop sub-categories to increase your authority in this product category and analyse the performance of new products brought into these sub-categories.

- Survey your customers and what problems your current merchandise solves. Their answers could surprise you and give you valuable ideas on new products to address those problems.

At the same time, it's also worth analysing which products to cull to make room for more profitable lines, by:

- Identifying those paid search terms on exact match 'eg oval mirrors' that convert poorly

- Examining products that have high rates of returns and refunds

- Ranking your products by sales and then looking at the least popular items at the bottom of the list to identify common themes

You can also gain clues from analysing your competitors' bestsellers and those in their clearance section. These relatively simple exercises put you in a strong position to put together a successful new product development programme.

Bestseller analysis – how to analyse bestsellers and their rate of decay

There is a circularity around bestsellers. They get to the top of the list precisely because they are innately desirable and large numbers of people want to buy them. That's important because these are the products that bring people to your site and trigger them to put the first product in their basket.

But what is a bestseller? Your criteria will depend on your particular business models, but Kevin Hillstrom[3] suggests making the cut at the top 5 per cent ranked by revenue and volume, and also the top 5 per cent ranked by volume alone.

Revenue and volume – these items bring in considerable revenue and also sell in large quantities.

Revenue alone – these items have a higher ticket price, so they generate considerable revenue but do not sell in such large quantities.

You'll often find that these few products make up over half of total sales so they are critical to the success of the business.

When you've split out your top sellers, simply count the actual number of bestsellers you've had in each of the last three years. It may look something like Table 6.2.

In this example, there has been a 36 per cent reduction in the number of bestsellers, down from 28 to 18. This decline represents a lost opportunity to promote desirable items to new and existing customers. Behind the scenes, the decline could also lead to reduced purchasing power with suppliers and erode margins.

With fewer product introductions and weaker performance of bestsellers this business needs to:

- ramp up the rate of new product introduction
- work on promoting existing items to bestseller status by marketing them better.

Table 6.2 Example count of bestsellers by year

Year	Number of items in 'bestsellers' categories
Year 1	28
Year 2	21
Year 3	18

Product category analysis

The way in which you organize and promote your product categories can have a significant impact on how well the products within those categories perform.

Some simple analysis will immediately tell you which categories generate the most product views, add-to-baskets, orders and revenue. Once you know this, you can see which categories perform well in terms of converting visitors into viewing them, adding to basket and finally paying for them. You can also perform this analysis to reposition categories in your navigation to increase sales.

To analyse the category performance just capture the following data:

1 **Category name** (eg sofas, lighting, kitchenware, etc).

2 **Category views**: number of visits to the site that included a visit to the particular category.

3 **Product views**: the number of times that any product page was viewed within the same visit as the particular category page was viewed.

4 **Baskets**: number of times that any product was added to the basket within the same visit as the category was viewed.

5 **Transactions**: number of transactions that took place in the same visit as the category was viewed.

6 **Revenue**: amount of revenue from orders placed in the same visit as the category was viewed.

Your analytics platform can probably produce this report for you, but if not, then simply fill in the data on a table similar to the example below. If your business has clear seasons separate this data into peak and non-peak time periods, otherwise the data captured should cover a calendar 12 months.

Table 6.3 Example of raw data required for Product Category Analysis

Category name	Category views	Product page views	Baskets	Trans-actions	Revenue
Category A	12,784	4,333	1,233	412	£22,933
Category B	15,898	3,736	1,112	598	£21,121
Category C	9,764	4,119	1,089	512	£18,083

Ratio analysis

Next use the raw data above to convert into ratios. These represent the performance of particular categories in terms of converting visitors into a product view, creating a basket and placing an order.

You now can sort the columns to produce the following views:

- Sort the **£ Per Category View** column with the highest £ at the top to identify those categories that generate the most revenue
- Sort the **Category: Transaction** column with the greatest number of orders at the top to identify those categories where propensity to buy is highest and lowest
- Sort the **Category: Basket** column with the highest at the top to identify those categories where propensity to add to basket is higher and lowest

While you get a clear overview of sales by category, you can study the visitors' journey through a category onto a product page, into the basket and then through the checkout at a more granular level. For a particular category, it may be that while overall 'sales per category view' are higher than for other categories, the ratio of baskets to order is relatively low.

This discovery means you have an opportunity to improve this part of the customer journey for a particular category. For example, if you were to compare categories containing higher-priced items (such as sofas) with lower-priced items (such as lighting), you may discover that while both categories had similar category: basket ratios, the sofa category had a much lower basket: order ratio.

In other words there is a barrier in the checkout part of the journey for sofa category visitors. This insight could prompt you to collect more data and take action to address the weaker performance in the checkout. For example, through using exit surveys, you may discover that delivery of large

Table 6.4   Ratios within product category data

Category: Name	Category: Product	Category: Basket	Category: Order	Baskets: Order	£ per Category view
Category A	33.9%	9.6%	3.2%	33.4%	£1.79
Category B	23.5%	7.0%	3.8%	53.8%	£1.33
Category C	42.2%	11.2%	5.2%	47.0%	£1.85

items like sofas is a key consideration for potential purchasers. You can then hypothesize that providing reassurance about the quality of your delivery service to these visitors at this point in their journey would increase their basket:order ratio and ultimately boost sales. A split test would give you the answer and, if you're right, you'll soon be selling more sofas.

Navigation analysis

You can also use this data to optimize the way you display categories in your navigation. In the example above, Category C has a much higher conversion rate to basket and order, and has the highest £ per category view.

Armed with this knowledge, you may want to consider putting Category C in a more prominent position in the navigation, promoting it through banners and moving products into Category C from other categories, provided they are a sensible fit.

Then just run a simple split-test to determine whether moving the high-performing category to a different place in the navigation gains additional sales.

Look-to-book analysis

Look-to-book is a nifty bit of analysis that helps you to identify a strategy for all your products based on the number of product page views and their add-to-basket ratio.

Originally devised by Bryan Eisenberg,[4] one of the earliest exponents of website optimization, this analysis is simple to do and yields great insights on your products, based on how your website visitors behave. First decide whether you are going to do seasonal analysis, such as peak and non-peak, or over a 12-month period.

To perform look-to-book analysis, you need the following information:

A. Total number of all unique product views (by unique visitor)

B. Total number of products (don't worry about individual SKUs, just the product lines)

C. Total number of unique views of the basket page (irrespective of whether the products end up being purchased or not)

D. Number of unique product views by product

E. Number of unique views of the basket page by product

This data will help you to produce two vital numbers:

- your average number of product page views
- your average add-to-basket ratio

Let's say you have 450 products and each page is viewed 350,000 times. Your average unique view per page is 777.

Your data says that your basket page gets 33,500 unique views. Dividing this by the total number of unique product page views (ie: 350,000) gives an average add-to-basket ratio of 9.5 per cent.

You now have two numbers:

- average product page views – 777
- average add-to-basket ratio – 9.5 per cent

Use them to benchmark every one of your products.

To calculate the add-to-basket ratio for each product, simply divide views of the basket when that product is in the basket with its number of page views.

Let's say that Product A has 1,100 unique page views and an add-to-basket ratio of 8.1 per cent.

- In terms of being viewed by your web visitors, it is above average (1,100 vs. 777).

- In terms of it being added to basket, it is below average (8.1 per cent vs. 9.5 per cent).

When you have done this for all of your products, the next step is to segment them into one of four segments as shown in the table below. HIGH means above average and LOW means below average.

Table 6.5 Segmenting each of your products

ID	Product page views	Add to basket ratio	What this means
A	HIGH (Above Average)	HIGH (Above Average)	These are your stars
B	HIGH (Above Average)	LOW (Below Average)	Visitors like the look of these products but don't buy. Why?
C	LOW (Below Average)	HIGH (Above Average)	These have hidden potential
D	LOW (Below Average)	LOW (Below Average)	These are the underperformers

Table 6.6 Product strategies after performing look-to-book analysis

	ID	LOW add-to-basket ratio	ID	HIGH add-to-basket ratio
HIGH product page views	B	Research and improve merchandising	A	Maintain or promote
LOW product page views	D	Remove or replace	C	Bundle with other products

This knowledge makes it very easy to decide which products to push (Segment A), which ones to get rid of (Segment D) and which ones need some attention (Segments B and C).

So what sort of attention should you give them?

For low-converting products that fall into segment B (high page views but low add-to-basket ratio), use online survey tools such as Qualaroo to understand why visitors are not adding items to their basket. Useful questions to ask include 'Is there any information missing on this product?' or more directly 'Why didn't you add this item to your basket?' The answers to this question will give you insight as to how you can better merchandise these products.

For high-converting products that fall into segment C (low product page views but high add-to-basket ratio) there is an opportunity to bundle products together with other bestsellers from segment A. This helps gets them noticed and can encourage visitors to place larger orders, which will increase your average order value.

In summary, use look-to-book analysis to develop a clear merchandising strategy for each one of your products based on the way your website visitors interact with them, as summarized below.

If you have a seasonal business with clear peak and non-peak periods, repeat this analysis for these two time frames as the products in each segment will change, and so will your strategy for each segment.

Price-point analysis

This useful form of analysis was born out of a pre-internet offline technique called SQUINCH or 'square inch analysis', used by catalogue marketers. They would quite literally measure exactly how much space was given to each product in the catalogue and divide it by the revenue generated to assess which ones were paying their way and which were taking up too much valuable room.

Table 6.7 Example of price-point analysis

Price point	Number of items offered	% of total items	No of orders containing items at this price point	% of total orders containing items at this price point	Variance
£0–£9.99	43	9.4%	6,230	9.0%	−0.3%
£10–£19.99	86	18.8%	9,561	13.9%	−4.9%
£20–£29.99	111	24.2%	17,665	25.6%	1.4%
£30–£34.99	80	17.5%	11,001	16.0%	−1.5%
£35–£39.99	65	14.2%	9,873	14.3%	0.1%
£40–£49.99	56	12.2%	7,892	11.5%	−0.8%
£50–£59.99	11	2.4%	4,332	6.3%	3.9%
>£60	6	1.3%	2,343	3.4%	2.1%
Total	458		68,897		

To perform modern day price-point analysis, firstly set out the total number of products at each price point. Ignore SKUs (eg colour and size variations) for the purposes of this analysis. The bands you use will depend on the spread of your product prices.

If you find that you have got a lot of products all bunched into one or two price bands, use smaller bands. In the example below, most of the price points are set at £10 intervals, but at £30 the bands are only £5 (£30–£34.99 and £35.00–£39.99). This was done to avoid bunching, because nearly a third of products fall into the £30–£39.99 band. Splitting this highly populated band into two gives a more even spread.

Then capture the total number of orders for all the items included in each price band. You can then work out the percentage for items offered and items ordered and the variance between the two.

Your table will probably look something like the example in Table 6.7.

Price-point analysis is designed to show you the price bands that your most popular products fall into. It is a message from your customers that gives a strong signal that you can offer them more items that cost that sort of price.

In the example above, we can see that items in the price band of £50–£59.99 make up just 2.5 per cent of total items offered but comprise 6.3 per cent of total sales. This is a firm indication that you can increase the number of items offered at this price point.

Conversely, the £10–£19.99 bracket accounts for 13.9 per cent of all sales but 18.8 per cent of all items. This is where you could look to reduce the number of items you sell.

However, do look at the bigger picture before delisting. Before making the final cut, check to see whether any of these items regularly appear in the first order a customer makes with you. Removing popular items for first-time orders could have a detrimental effect on your ability to convert new visitors into first-time buyers.

Price testing

As a rule of thumb, as the price increases, demand falls. However, people will almost always pay more for something, if it's presented in the right way. The problem is that you never really know how much more unless you engage in some form of price testing.

It's unreliable to simply ask people what they would be prepared to pay; consumers are notorious for saying one thing but doing another.

As the pioneering ad agency founder David Ogilvy asserted, 'Customers don't know what they feel, don't say what they know, and don't do what they say. Market research is three steps removed from real behaviour.'[5]

Therefore in order to understand how much you can charge for your products – or their demand elasticity – without losing sales, quantitative testing is more reliable.

There are a number of ways you can do this, including increasing your prices and analysing the sales before and after the price increase. However, with this method it is difficult to trust the results because there could be several other factors at play.

There is a way to use a scientific approach to price testing and discover the maximum price you can charge for selected products without harming overall demand. The last few years have seen the launch of a number of price-testing tools, including WisePricer, Visual Website Optimizer and Tatvic.

Tatvic, for example, offers a service called LiftSuggest which allows you to test one or more different prices to a proportion of your website visitors. You can then compare sales on both the higher- and lower-priced groups and see whether the higher price makes a difference. Although it's not actually illegal to offer the same product at two or more different prices at once, it's generally considered immoral and consumers are outraged if they discover it.

To avoid negatives of this kind, LiftSuggest reduces the price at the last minute for the customer. It does this by showing the higher price on the

Figure 6.1   Example of price reduction after higher-priced item has been added to basket

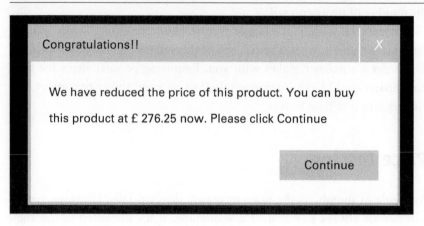

category and product pages only. Once the visitor has added the product to the basket they are shown a message that tells them how to reduce the cost to get the lower price such as, '*Your price has been reduced by £x. Please click OK to continue.*'

The LiftSuggest reporting dashboard lets you see whether the add-to-basket ratio of the product offered at the higher price is different to the product offered at the base price. You may find that pricing a product 10 per cent higher does not lower the add-to-basket ratio but when you price it 15 per cent higher there is a reduction. This will give you the confidence that increasing your product's price by 10 per cent will not harm sales. Price testing in this way can also be used to evaluate the impact of cutting prices to see whether a lower price results in higher levels of gross margin.

Revenue optimization is a key part of optimizing your website. Price testing helps avoid underpricing (where you give away too much margin) and overpricing (where you lose sales because the price puts too many people off). Either way, when you price test in an objective and scientific way, you'll optimize your revenue – a key part of website optimization.

Summary

Merchandising analytics is a range of valuable research techniques for website optimization. They give you useful insights into the interaction between your visitors, the merchandise you offer and the actions your visitors take.

Using merchandising analytics allows you to determine the impact on sales of a declining rate of new product introduction, and how a fall in revenue from bestsellers over time could damage your business. Category analysis identifies poorly performing categories as well as the chance to understand underlying reasons. You can optimize your navigation for higher sales by examining which categories result in higher and lower levels of conversion and revenue. Look-to-book analysis is a simple and easy way to develop a strategy for each of your products based on the number of views they receive and how likely it is they are added to your basket. Using price-point analysis enables you to scientifically pinpoint where you have authority to sell more products in this price band, and those that could be culled without damaging sales. Price testing gives you the opportunity to determine the maximum selling price without reducing order volume.

For e-commerce businesses selling products, merchandising analytics is a vital part of the research stage and worth repeating on a regular eg six-monthly or seasonal basis.

Notes

1 Hillstrom, K (2013) Hillstrom's Merchandise Forensics: A Case Study In Understanding Why Merchandising Issues Impact Marketing Productivity And Business Health, CreateSpace Independent Publishing Platform, USA.

2 Hillstrom, K (2013) Hillstrom's Merchandise Forensics: A Case Study In Understanding Why Merchandising Issues Impact Marketing Productivity And Business Health, CreateSpace Independent Publishing Platform, USA.

3 Hillstrom, K (2013) Hillstrom's Merchandise Forensics: A Case Study In Understanding Why Merchandising Issues Impact Marketing Productivity And Business Health, CreateSpace Independent Publishing Platform, USA.

4 Eisenberg, B and Eisenberg, J (2005) Call to Action, Wizard Academy Press, Austin, Texas.

5 Ogilvy, D (1985) Ogilvy on Advertising, Vintage, New York.

Creating the optimization plan

07

Data is pouring in from various sources. It's exciting, but can be daunting. You might feel like you're drowning in figures and survey responses. So where do you start? How do you distil insights from all of this, and then mould them into a list of experiments?

The answer is to create an Optimization Plan. Start by sifting through the data, noting all your ideas and observations in a spreadsheet or similar. At this stage, it is little more than just a log of ideas for tests, in no particular order. Soon, you'll order and prioritize this list, at which point it becomes an actionable plan.

Ideation

Ideation is the process of generating ideas, which happens as you are combing through the data. It has two components, analysis and synthesis. They happen hand in hand all the time as you work with the data. Analysis is breaking down data into smaller parts, pieces of the puzzle you're trying to solve. Synthesis is when you tie it all together – like joining up the dots to complete the puzzle. It is when you turn your observations into insights, which leads to the ideas about what you might want to test.

Note down all ideas and observations as you go through the data. It will be a disjointed list in jumbled order, but trust that a picture will gradually start forming. Go with the process; don't expect to know what to test until you've done all the analysis. Don't rush into conclusions prematurely. Some of the ideas may never materialize, but it's vital to jot down each one as it is born. You will almost certainly forget it unless it's captured somewhere.

A spreadsheet works well for this purpose, and that same document can gradually be expanded to become your Optimization Plan. Typically you will have a row for each idea with columns for notes, the area of the site, and the data that led you to the idea. Later you may add other column headings such as Stage and Priority to help track each idea as it works its way through the process. An example is shown in Table 7.1. There the letters relate to data sources such as S for Survey, U for Usability, L for Live Chat and so on. At this point, it only contains raw ideas, as they come up. Later they will be ranked in order of priority.

When working with data, analysis paralysis is a common trap, but you can avoid it. Just be clear: your task is not to squeeze every last drop of intelligence out of every tiny bit of data. At some point, the additional gain doesn't justify the additional effort.

You don't need to chain yourself to a huge pile of reports and read every number and every word. Dip, not dive, into each data source, and set a limited time for each one. Make Parkinson's Law, 'Work expands so as to fill the time available for its completion',[1] act in your favour. Simply by budgeting a strict (and short) time for a task, you can avoid analysis paralysis.

Of course, you have to be reasonable. Can you produce a segmented funnel map in five minutes? No, but you probably don't need five hours

Table 7.1 Example of an Optimization Plan at the ideation stage. The letters relate to data sources such as S for Survey, U for Usability, L for Live Chat and so on. At this point, it only contains raw ideas, as they come up. Later they will be ranked in order of priority

Idea	Notes	Area	Source				
			S	U	L	I	Q
Introduce 'Add to Cart' buttons on PLP	High incidence of pogo-sticking observed; one user suggested having 'Add to Cart' would be useful	PLP	1	1	1		1
Demote 'Voucher Code' box on basket page	Test users are leaving the basket to hunt for vouchers in Google	Basket Page	1				1
Main navigation	Not easy to find XYZ product just by looking at the menu	Main Nav		1			

either. Depending on the task and your prior experience with it, allow yourself one or two hours initially. Three hours tops. You can always come back to it at a later point, by which time you'll have more context from having seen a wider range of data. You'll be better informed and more focused when you loop back to a data source.

So do just enough to pull out key insights. No more. How do you know what point is enough? At first new insights will be coming thick and fast, but soon the same ones will be popping up again and again. You'll quickly get an idea of recurring themes, and that may signal it's time to stop.

Suppose for example you have thousands of responses to an on-site poll. There's no need to put every single response under the microscope. Start with around 200 randomly selected responses to categorize and sort. That will enable you to identify and rank the themes, and get a good overview of what this particular source has to offer. If you feel you are still getting surprised by some of the responses after 200, then do another 100 – although chances are that won't happen.

In a short space of time, you'll end up with a list of potential candidates for split testing. It doesn't matter how long the list is. Later on, these ideas are put in order, and at that point it becomes your fully formed Optimization Plan.

Key to successful ideation is your ability to turn data into ideas. How do you go about generating the ideas that go into your plan? Here are some techniques we have found helpful:

- Massaging the data
- Visualizing
- Triangulating
- Categorizing
- 5 Whys (root cause analysis)
- Insight review

Massaging the data

It's easy to become overwhelmed by the sheer volume of data sitting on your desk, waiting to be processed. Break it down into small chunks that seem more manageable. Like the cliché says – the way to eat an elephant is one bite at a time. Ideation is largely about just playing with data.

It's as simple as it sounds. Pick a data source, load it into a spreadsheet and try different ways of manipulating it to see what jumps out at you. Sum, average, calculate differences and proportions, make pivot tables, sort, do comparisons and so on. Google Analytics (GA) is a good place to start sniffing around. But don't get so carried away that you forget to diligently log observations, patterns and trends.

Visualization aids interpretation

Graphs and charts are powerful ways to make sense of data. With each piece of analysis, ask yourself if there is anything you can represent visually.

- **Pie charts** are best for comparing the parts of a whole, such as new vs returning visitors.

- **Bar charts** are good for comparing different groups of data like themed survey answers, or page templates in a customer journey map.

- **Line graphs** are the best way of plotting and comparing trends over time such as how your conversion rate and revenue have changed over 12 months.

For now, don't worry about making the graph look pretty. Your goal is to visualize that data so you can quickly see the links and trends. The visuals don't go into the Optimization Plan – it's just a technique that helps you to identify ideas to pursue. Hang on to them though. Later on, they may come in handy when you present findings to stakeholders.

Triangulate different data sources

Scientists often use more than one research method to investigate the same concept from different angles. It's a powerful technique, known as triangulation. To evolve an idea, look for ways in which to add dimensions to it by bringing data from different sources to bear on that idea.

It is especially useful to triangulate qualitative and quantitative research. Qualitative research is a rich source of new ideas. The advantage of quantitative research is that you can express in numbers the observations underpinning that idea. A new dimension is added to it by ordering, ranking, comparing etc. It makes for a perfect marriage between qualitative and quantitative data. Use the strengths of each to shine a light on the idea from different angles.

Sometimes triangulation will happen naturally. Other times you'll have to work at it. Imagine that during usability testing, a user abandons the basket page because of delivery costs. What is the exit rate of this page in GA? What do heatmaps tell you about where people click on the basket page – on the 'delivery info' link perhaps? If so, what happens once users reach that page? What other data sources could be used to build on this observation? Can you fire up a quick onsite poll on that page to examine this issue further?

This is the kind of thing that may not get picked up if different people are looking at different data. If one person does all the research and analysis, they are best placed to make the judgements and tie everything together. If it's a team, then there needs to be coordination and a process for feeding all the distilled insights from each person to an overseer who holds the role of a single controlling intelligence.

Categorize

To help you break up that haystack of information into more manageable heaps, create virtual piles around certain themes. Start by sorting the individual items into categories; themes will reveal themselves to you as you progress. It's how you start to see links and connections between ideas. It also lets you identify the bigger issues and rank them in order of importance.

For example, when reviewing responses to the question 'What were your initial fears and concerns about buying from us?' you may find that comments fit into categories such as the following:

- Delivery timeframe (questions around how long it will take to receive the item)
- Touch and feel (not being able to see item before buying it)
- Damage (will it arrive in one piece?)

Ask 'Why?' five times

This is a popular technique known as the Five Whys. It comes under the umbrella of root cause analysis, a specialized analytical framework to identify the core of a problem. There are many ways to get to the core – this

Table 7.2   The Five Whys technique applied to an investigation into low mobile conversion rates

Iteration	Answer	Data source
First Why	Our mobile visitors don't buy as frequently as desktop visitors.	Analytics
Second Why	Mobile visitors browse more than desktop visitors.	Analytics
Third Why	Those same visitors are buying on desktop.	External research report
Fourth Why	It is more convenient for them to browse on mobile.	Usability Testing / Interview
Fifth Why	They are multi-tasking and distractible when visiting on mobile, whereas on desktop the experience is more focused.	Usability Testing / Mobile poll

framework is one of the easiest. State the problem, then ask why this is the case. Repeat until you get to the root cause, as shown in Table 7.2.

As you ask the next question, you may realize that you need further data in order to give an informed response. This will guide your efforts. Even if you lack relevant data on which to base your answers, it can be the start of a hypothesis to test or it can be flagged for further research and analysis.

As an example, let's say you're investigating low mobile conversion rates. The process could develop as illustrated below.

Insight review

At the end of each day, review what you've learnt up until that point. Revisit your most interesting or insightful graphs. What is the story that's taking shape? How has it changed since the last review? Are there any obvious gaps in the story so far? If you're working in a team, looking at different data sources, find a way of coordinating this so that every researcher is fully up to speed.

Sorting the ideas in the optimization plan

Once you have gone through all your data and logged all your ideas, you can start prioritizing everything with a view to putting your test programme in place.

First make a YES/NO decision about whether the idea is sufficiently formed to consider testing it immediately. YES ideas go into the Wireframe bucket, where they will be ranked. Next they will be built, focusing on the most promising ones first, launched into a split test and eventually the test is concluded. For each of these stages, there is a bucket (Figure 7.1).

Some ideas will need more work before they can be considered for testing. They may need to be investigated or developed further, or you may have to take technical measures to collect relevant data. These ideas that are not yet ready to be wireframed go into your pipeline.

There is also a separate category known as JDI (Just Do It). Some things are so obviously plain wrong that they don't need to be tested, they need to be put right. These should go straight to the web developers with clear instructions on what needs to be fixed. Examples include browser and/or device compatibility issues and bugs.

This process of bucketing and sorting the ideas is shown on the flowchart below.

A breakdown of the buckets follows:

Test? Yes

Your 'yes' ideas go into the Wireframe bucket, to be tested first. Obviously you can't test them all at once, so the order in which they are done will be decided later through a formal process of prioritization, described later in this chapter.

Figure 7.1 Buckets will help you keep track of ideas as they work their way through the process from ideation through testing to conclusion

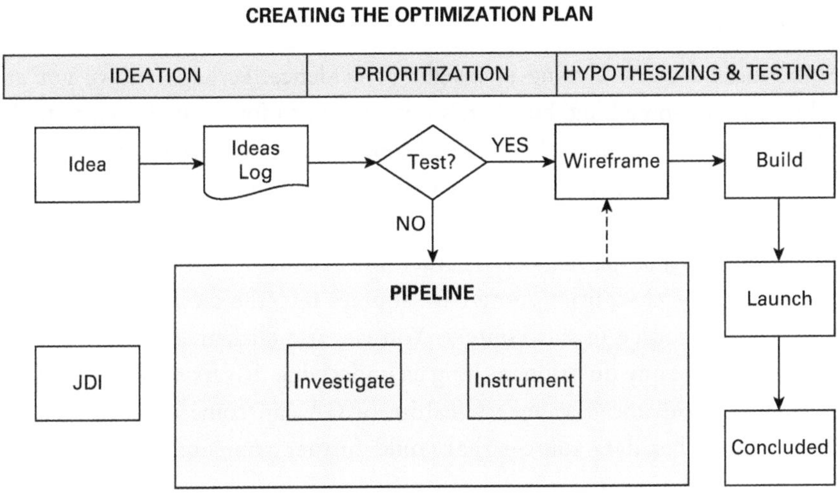

CREATING THE OPTIMIZATION PLAN

They then move through the system from one bucket to another:

Build

As the wireframe and test spec are submitted to the web developers for coding, that idea is parked here. Having it all in one place could help you to make more effective use of development resources.

Launch

Move the idea here when you start testing it. This gives you visibility of everything that is currently live, and can show whether you are making best use of your available testing slots. This is discussed in Chapter 9.

Concluded

The final bucket, used for all tests that have been completed. When an experiment is concluded, it is not the end as we explain in Chapter 9. Strictly speaking, this just refers to the test having been ended.

Test? No

As mentioned above, the ideas which are not ready to be tested go into your pipeline. (This is what your tech people may call 'the backlog'). They are placed in one of three buckets:

- Investigate
- Instrument
- Develop

Investigate

Some ideas may be lacking in insight or evidence. Perhaps you've got an inkling about something, but there's not enough to formulate into a testable idea. This is one instance where the judgement of the optimizer counts – being able to recognize when there's a twinkling of an idea in a passing comment for example, and being open to finding out more. You may therefore need to do further analysis, perhaps even gather more data.

If this is the case, bring more data sources into the picture. GA is often a fantastic resource in this context. You can use clickstream data to shed light on almost any question, as long as underlying drivers are tracked. This is where the advanced segments feature of GA can come in handy. Think also about other data sources that could further your understanding. For example, is there an unexplored angle in heatmaps, session recordings or survey data?

Split testing itself can also be a source of evidence and insight. A narrowly targeted test could help you establish the conversion potential of an idea or site element. The caveat is that it should not be done at the expense of the roadmap. This is discussed in more detail in Chapter 9.

Instrument

In certain cases, you may not yet have the right tools deployed in order to collect the necessary data. It could be that some additional configuration has to be done in GA, or it might be time to install a new tool to properly investigate an issue.

We recently worked with a major retailer where a vast number of product lines were fitted into the site's main navigation. There were indications that this was an area that had to be optimized, but we needed some more data on it to ascertain exactly what the size of the opportunity was. We employed Treejack and Optimal Sort, online tools perfect for this purpose, but not a standard part of our kit.

Internal ideas submission form

Inviting your colleagues to contribute ideas can help promote buy-in. Some companies even offer prizes for the most impactful ideas. One way to do this is by submission form in Google Forms, asking for at least:

- Name of submitter
- Idea to test
- Thoughts about what led to the idea

Just as when you conduct a brainstorming, there are no rules at this stage. Be open and receptive to any ideas that are generated. Nobody has a monopoly on inspiration. Allow all ideas through, no matter how unconvincing or unsubstantiated they seem at first glance. You will have the chance to filter out the subjective opinions and wild guesses later.

In fact it's common to get a lot of strongly-held but completely subjective opinions from your internal colleagues. Do let them come into the system, as long as your contributors know that everything will be filtered by the same prioritization process. Their ideas might not be next in line just yet.

The Optimization Plan is never set in stone. It could change at any point as new insights come to light. These may come from a range of sources:

- Reprioritization of ideas
- Insights from concluded split tests
- New data not previously available
- Previous research re-examined
- New techniques for data analysis
- New people in your organization with fresh ideas

Keeping track of it all

Moving ideas from initial observation to conclusion via the various buckets requires some organization. You can do it all with spreadsheets and a card sorter like Trello, which are free. Check out Smartsheet, a low-cost project management tool with spreadsheets, card sorter and resource management capabilities.

There are also specialist CRO project management tools such as Effective Experiments, Experiment Engine and Iridion. As Effective Experiments founder Manuel da Costa, an experienced optimizer in his own right, explains: "Running an optimization programme is time consuming work with analysing data and running tests. We found that teams were becoming inefficient and unable to keep track of everything that was going on." These bespoke tools can make things easier by integrating roadmapping, project management and reporting into one platform.

How to prioritize ideas

As you've seen above, ideation will easily yield dozens, if not hundreds, of ideas to explore. You've made the first cut and sent the ideas that need more work into your pipeline for later.

This will still leave you with a host of ideas ready for wireframing. But where do you start? You can't test everything all at once so what do you test first? What can you safely ignore for the time being and come back to later?

Prioritizing your ideas is one of the most important pieces of the puzzle, because, as Bill Gates says, 'Prioritization is effectiveness.'[2]

Clearly the ones you should be wanting to do first are those that you think will get the highest revenue uplifts for the least amount of effort. Unfortunately that's impossible to predict. Even experienced optimizers get this wrong. Whilst there is no crystal ball to tell you exactly which ones will win, there are ways to identify which are more likely to do better, and it's these you want to bump to the top of the list.

At this stage you have a choice about how you make that call. You can rank everything according to some logical principles. Or you can randomly work through the list, picking the ones you like the sound of or that seem easy to do. This is referred to in the industry as RATS (Random Acts of Testing). It's surprisingly common, but it's no better than playing the lottery and is a real waste of your valuable time.

The team at Optimost proved this when they randomly picked tests out of a successful optimization project. Most tests only saw measly uplifts and didn't reflect the overall success of the project.[3] Their experiment illustrates why it's worth spending time identifying the ideas with the highest ROI (Return on Investment) potential. So there is real value in taking the time to rank your list in order of priority, using a system based on objective criteria.

There are several systems used by CRO practitioners to carry out prioritization, including the well-known PIE framework by Chris Goward, the Time-Impact-Resources model by Bryan Eisenberg and the Additive System recommended by the testing platform Optimizely.[4]

The model we use at AWA was developed by our optimization team, and incorporates elements from all these frameworks. We call it EPE, which is short for Evidence, Potential and Ease and also sounds like épée, a sword used in fencing to get to your target and win.

Evidence-Potential-Ease framework

Score each idea 1–5 on three different criteria namely Evidence, Potential and Ease, using Table 7.3 as a guide.

Evidence

At core, the system advocated in this book is about avoiding instinct, and instead following an objective, data-led approach. You will have gone to great lengths to gather evidence in support of your testing ideas; now it's time to weigh it all up. The weight of evidence, and strength of that evidence, will vary. For each item on the list, ask: How much evidence do you have for this? What is the quality of that evidence?

Table 7.3   An easy system for ranking your ideas

Score	Potential	Evidence	Ease
★★★★★ There can only be a few of these.	Very high potential, such as critical usability issues with high occurrence rate, in area where high drop-off is observed. Situated in an area of the site with high traffic and relatively high contribution to total revenue.	Strong evidence from multiple sources points to it being an issue or opportunity.	The test is easy to code and implement. It enjoys the full support of everyone in the organization.
★★★★	High potential, such as a critical usability issue or characterized by a high drop-off rate. May occur in an area of the site with slightly less traffic or where contribution to revenue is slightly lower.	At least one strong source of evidence.	The test is easy to code. It enjoys the support of most people in the organization.
★★★	Medium potential, such as a usability issue ranked Medium, or one with a lower occurrence rate. Could also be high potential idea in an area of the site where there is less traffic or smaller contribution to revenue.	At least one source of evidence.	The test is relatively easy to code. It enjoys wide support in the organization.
★★	Medium to low potential idea in area of the site with low traffic or low contribution to revenue. Could be a usability issue marked Low.	May have only one source of evidence, or weak evidence.	Relatively complex to code. Or idea does not have wide support in the organization.
★	Low potential, occurring in areas with low traffic.	Weak evidence, or no objective evidence.	Ideas that are difficult to implement should fall in this category, even if it has higher potential.

The number one way of evaluating strength of evidence is to consider how many different data sources point to one particular area. Say for example that usability testing unearthed a potentially important observation, but it only affected one user. Without further evidence, it's difficult to assign high priority to that issue.

However, if you also have Google Analytics (GA) data pointing to the same issue, you have reason to increase its priority. As more data sources lend weight to the observation, it increases in importance. The more corroborating evidence there is, the higher the evidence score should be.

This is why it's useful to cross-reference the data sources against each idea on your list. Looking back at Table 7.1 above, it's easy to see that Idea 1 is the one with most evidence behind it. Simply create a Total column and add up all the 1's in each row.

It's however also important to consider the quality of evidence behind each idea. A whimsical internal suggestion cannot carry the same weight as something based on objective evidence.

Potential

Assessing potential implies a degree of judgment, but that should not be completely subjective. Make it as objective as you can, by taking into account the factors below.

- Funnel drop-off rate
- Severity of usability issue
- Quantitative indicators
- Distance to conversion
- Traffic exposure
- Testable population

Funnel drop-off rate

This is a big broad-brush indicator of where to start focusing your efforts. When you created your journey maps (see Chapter 4), you saw where visitors are leaking from the funnel. Theoretically, the areas where the biggest drop-offs occur should give you the biggest impacts when you change them for the better.

Be warned though that it's not always this straightforward, unfortunately. For example, on most e-commerce sites, the biggest leak will be on the Product Detail Page (PDP). Does this mean that the PDP presents the biggest opportunity? Or does it merely reflect normal behaviour such as shopping around, gathering information and post-purchase activity. You have to view it in the context of other data. If, for example, you had evidence from usability testing of mass confusion at that point in the journey, it would then add to the weight of this opportunity.

Severity of usability issue

We explained how to rank each usability issue in terms of severity in Chapter 4. For example, High represents a showstopper. Clearly, this information is directly relevant to prioritization.

Quantitative indicators

These help you decide which ideas are worth taking more seriously. There are a number of quantitative metrics you can use to give you a steer, and here are some of the most useful:

Bounce Rate / Exit Rate

Both Bounce Rate and Exit Rate are measures in GA of the rate at which visitors leave the site from the page in question. A bounce is when someone enters the site, but leaves without taking any action on that page. An exit happens when the visitor leaves after having seen at least one other page on the site prior to the one from which they leave. Keep in mind that everyone has to exit the site at some point, so exclude outliers and check how ratios compare to the average.

Page Value

Page Value in GA measures the monetary value of the last page a user visited before completing the transaction. How does the page or template in question compare to the average? It it's lower than average, that may be a signal that the page presents a bigger opportunity. Strip out any outliers when calculating the average by setting parameters using GA's inline filtering.

Occurrence rate of observations

If the issue was observed during usability testing, how frequently did it occur? What percentage of people in the study were affected by it?

Distance to conversion

The further away an event is from the point at which your visitors convert, the less direct influence it has on that conversion. For example, the 'Add to Basket' button on a Product Detail Page (PDP) is further away from a purchase than 'Proceed to Checkout' on the basket page. The effect of that 'Add to Basket' micro conversion could be so small that it's washed away in aggregate numbers. As you move higher up the funnel, you may have to track these micro conversions, like number of clicks on an element, rather than macro conversions such as purchase conversion rate or Revenue Per Visitor (RPV). The problem with that is that your bank won't accept clicks on an element; you can only deposit money.

If you report on RPV, you should consider line of sight between the experience being tested and revenue generation. Work out the contribution to overall revenue of the page template where the test will be run. Let's take the homepage as an example. Use GA to create an advanced segment for homepage views (see Chapter 4). Then compare this segment against the default *All Sessions* segment in the *Ecommerce Overview* report. This will show you how much homepage viewers added to your revenue in the given period, as in Table 7.2:

Traffic exposure

What percentage of visitors are exposed to the area in question? The length of time you have to run at test for depends on how many people visit that page where the test is active (traffic volume). The further down the funnel you go, the lower the traffic. Nearly all your customers see the global header, only some will see a category page, and even fewer will make it to the Product Detail Page (PDP). Therefore a test on the PDP will have a smaller sample size than a test on the global header.

Where on the page the change is introduced also makes a difference. Scroll maps can be helpful to determine how far down a page your visitors reach. Say you want to treat an element in the lower half of a page template. GA tells you that the page receives 50,000 visitors per month. Sounds good!

Figure 7.2   The advanced segment for homepage views compared to all sessions

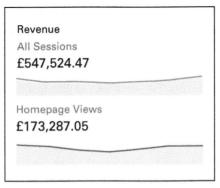

NOTE £173,287/£547,524 = 31.6%. So in this case, homepage viewers contributed only about a third to overall revenue in the period under review. Any RPV result that you achieve from running a test on the homepage, would have to be divided by 31.6% to arrive at the true site-wide revenue impact (see Chapter 9)

However, from the scroll maps you know that only 20 per cent of those visitors scroll down far enough to see that section of the page. Your available sample for this experiment is suddenly sliced from 50k to 10k visitors!

Testable population

The nature of some experiments is such that they only target a subsection of pages, or a subsection of the overall population.

Continuing the PDP scenario above, say your test involves showing a big 'SAVE' flash next to any discounted product. Unless every product is marked down, the available sample shrinks, as the flash will only be shown on some PDPs, not all.

Alternatively, suppose you have identified an opportunity only accessible to logged-in users, such as the wishlisting feature. You'd have to then consider what percentage of your test population is logged in, or willing to create an account. If they aren't then you won't be able to get them in the experiment.

Ease

Ease refers to both how easy it is to build the split test, and how feasible or easy it would be for the organization to implement it within the business.

Technical resources are stretched in every organization. The average split test should take no more than a few hours to code, but if it's a complex test, it could take a lot longer. Before tying up costly engineering capacity in building a complex experiment, you want to be sure that it's going to deliver the goods.

Since it's impossible to predict the outcome of a test, the next best thing is to assign these harder-to-build tests to a lower priority. It doesn't mean you won't get to it, but don't let it clog up your test pipeline at the start of a programme, when it's important to be building momentum.

Also take into account whether the company could actually implement the change if the test wins. For example, if you test giving your customers one-hour delivery slots but your business can't actually achieve that, then it can't be urgent.

Complexities can also be political in nature. You may have to fight to bring some experiments to life. Expect others to push back on certain ideas. Over time, as you build up credibility, any resistance should ease. Until then, pick your battles wisely.

The homepage in particular is often considered sacrosanct within an organization. A web team at a well-known fashion retailer believed their homepage was rich in potential, but were at odds with their marketing department who were concerned that testing would result in 'hard sell' messages that would dilute the brand.

They were won round later, when they saw for themselves the value of split testing brings. They became excited about learning new things and removing opinions from the debate and agreed for the homepage to become a testing ground.

We have even heard rumours that a giant international brand would sometimes exclude their company's internal IP address range from experiments to limit the chances of colleagues seeing the changes!

The Additive System

The Additive System is a different way of prioritizing the list to turn your ideas log into an actionable plan. You may find this method more suitable if you need a greater degree of control and flexibility than other frameworks allow.

As an example, it is common to be under pressure from senior people in the organization to run a test even when there is no strong evidence that it's likely to get an uplift. Putting a test in the queue, simply because the CEO wants to run it, could undermine your optimization efforts, and ultimately your results. There is also a lost opportunity cost. You have finite resources, so time and effort spent on it blocks the chance to run one that could have achieved sizeable gain. Ultimately if you're forced to 'just do it' you have no real choice. The Additive System allows you to take that into account by, for example, adding a consideration for strategic importance.[5]

To use the Additive System, first create a list of considerations relevant to your situation. Then add 1 point if the consideration satisfies the condition, and zero points if it doesn't satisfy this condition. An example can be seen in Table 7.4.

You may adapt this to your own needs and use your own labels. Don't be too zealous though as it can become a daunting exercise having to run through a long list of considerations. On the other hand, if you have too few points of reference in the table, then you may end up with several ideas that have the same score.

Table 7.4 The Additive System – an alternative method of prioritizing ideas within your Optimization Plan

Consideration	Add +1 Point if...	Give 0 Points if...
Primary Metric = RPV	It is possible to track RPV as a primary metric	RPV can't be supported as a primary metric
High Attrition Area	Targets an area of the site that has a high drop-off rate	Targets an area of the site that doesn't have high attrition
Bounce Rate / Exit Rate	The target page or template has a high Bounce Rate and/or Exit Rate	Bounce Rate and/or Exit Rate is average or below average
Page Value	The target page or template has a relatively high Page Value	Page Value is average or below average
Occurrence Rate	The issue was observed more than once in usability testing	The issue was observed once only, or not at all
Severity of Issue	During usability testing, the issue was found to get in the way of conversions	The issue was a minor irritation at best, but would not block a conversion
Traffic Exposure	The page has enough traffic to meet sample size requirements	There is not enough traffic to meet sample size requirements
Testable Population	The test does not target an element which appears on a subsection of pages, or to a subsection of visitors	The test targets an area that is limited to a subsection of pages and/or visitors
Fold	Targets an area of the page which is visible to all or most visitors	Scroll maps show the target area is not visible to everyone
Ease	The test is relatively easy to build and/or implement	The test is not easy to build and/or implement
Evidence	Supported by two or more credible sources of evidence	Backed by only one source

These are just two systems that you can use, and you may find that you want to adapt them or develop something that suits your business model better. The important thing is to prioritize. Any system is better than nothing.

What started as a blank spreadsheet is now a valuable roadmap for your testing programme with ideas ready to go, and a bank of ideas in the pipeline.

Summary

The Optimization Plan houses all your ideas for split tests, and helps you to keep track of where each idea is in the process.

It starts life as an unordered ideas log, where you jot down every idea as it comes to you. To generate ideas, you go through a process known as ideation. This involves sifting through all your data to mine insights from it. Techniques to help you pull the strands together to get a complete picture include massing, triangulating and visualizing the data.

The first stage for any mature idea is the Wireframe bucket. A formal hypothesis statement is written and wireframe created. It will then pass through various buckets until the experiment has run and concluded.

Ideas that are not ready for Wireframing go into the pipeline. To bring them on, it may be necessary to investigate the data in more depth (Investigate bucket), or put extra research tools on the site to find out more (Instrument bucket).

Once you have a list of ideas, it is crucial to prioritize them. It has been proven that randomly picking ideas produces inferior results.

Two methods that can be used for this are the EPE framework and the Additive System. EPE aims to remove subjectivity from the decision as far as possible, whereas the Additive System is flexible and adaptable to suit your organization's needs. You are now ready to start running your first split tests.

Notes

1 The Economist (1955) Parkinson's law. Available from: http://www.economist. com/node/14116121 (Accessed: 1 July 2016).

2 BBC (2016) Bill Gates, *Desert Island Discs*, BBC Radio 4. Available from: http://www.bbc.co.uk/programmes/b06z1zdt (Accessed: 1 July 2016).

3 Kogan, U, O'Malley, D, Warner, A (2016) Game-changing CRO in four quarters. [Webinar]. Available from: https://www.whichtestwon.com/ wp-content/uploads/2016/03/HP-WTW-Game-Changing-CRO.pdf (11 February 2016).

4 Rusonis, S (2015) A method for Prioritizing A/B test ideas that won't hurt feelings. Available from: https://blog.optimizely.com/2015/05/05/how-to-prioritize-ab-testing-ideas/ (Accessed: 1 July 2016).

5 Rusonis, S (2015) A method for Prioritizing A/B test ideas that won't hurt feelings. Available from: https://blog.optimizely.com/2015/05/05/how-to-prioritize-ab-testing-ideas/ (Accessed: 1 July 2016).

Hypotheses and creative work

08

What is a hypothesis?

If split testing is at the heart of successful website optimization, good hypotheses are key to ongoing success. It's what makes the difference between a high-performing optimization programme and simply doing lots of A/B testing.

A formally developed hypothesis statement means you are truly focused on the customer and their needs. That means you are much more likely to test something meaningful that gets results. A well-formulated hypothesis also helps you to learn something new about your customers with each test.

A hypothesis is a prediction that making certain changes to your website will result in an increase in sales. This is based on evidence about customer behaviour and feedback. When you test those changes, your primary Key Performance Indicator (KPI) goes up or down. If it goes up, your hypothesis is found to be valid.

As Flint McLaughlin, MD of online research group, MECLABS, states, 'The goal of a test is not to get a lift, but rather to get a learning.' It is the hypothesis that enables you to learn from an experiment, even if it is negative. If your KPI goes down, you can look to your hypothesis to enhance your understanding of the problem you were trying to treat. The negative result tells you that the variable being tested caused visitors to behave in a different way than you expected. Why? When you think through the possible reasons for this, you will be able to revise your hypothesis accordingly and then run another test. Very often, the enhanced knowledge you now have will get you a different result next time.

Suppose for example you've noticed that people who use your site search box convert at a much higher rate than non-searchers. This leads you to hypothesize that increasing the prominence of your search box will lead to more visitors conducting site searches, which will increase revenue. The experiment measures the outcome in terms of Revenue Per Visitor (RPV) and total number of searches conducted.

It's possible that after the test you see that the number of searches increased, but revenue actually went down. This could mean a number of things. One explanation might be that browsing and discovery are more important for your visitors than you realized. You could then revise the hypothesis, for example, to one promoting inspirational paths.

Optimization expert Craig Sullivan expresses these three core components of a CRO hypothesis in the following framework:

'Because we observed data [A] and feedback [B], we believe that doing [C] for people [D] will make outcome [E] happen. We'll know this when we observe data [F] and obtain feedback [G]'.[1]

So what does a hypothesis look like in real life? Here is an example.

Sector: Homewares, merchandise bought on credit

Because we observed [A] analytics data, which indicated there was a large drop-off between the product and basket page and heatmap analysis showed a large volume of clicks on the product images [B], feedback from usability testers centred on concerns about whether they could afford the repayments and wanted to know if there was some kind of 'deal' available. Users also queried which items were included in a bedding set. We believed that by [C] making the finance calculator more visible, setting the most popular bedding set as the default option and making the images larger and offering a pop-up to View the Bedding Set with a full list of items [D] for all visitors would [E] increase RPV.

Sometimes your tests are big and bold, and at other times they are small and iterative. As we discuss in Chapter 9, small changes are less likely to get the 'big win', but you will learn more precisely the impact of a single change. A balance between big, bold tests and small, iterative ones is crucial.

From hypothesis to creative work

Once you have formally stated your hypothesis, there are then five steps to follow to get material ready to run the split test:

1 Create wireframe and copy

2 Review wireframe and copy

3 Create the artwork

4 Review the artwork

5 Hand over creative to development

Step One: Create wireframe and copy

Wireframe

A wireframe is the bare bones of the web page, or web experience, shown as a mock-up of the proposed layout of the new page (or pages) you want to test. Typically it is a simple line drawing with finished copy and unfinished images (see example below). This lack of polish helps to keep the focus on the core functionality and variables that are intended to change behaviour. What matters is that the wireframe clearly shows key elements needed to fulfil the requirements of the hypothesis.

Figure 8.1 Example of lo-fi wireframe

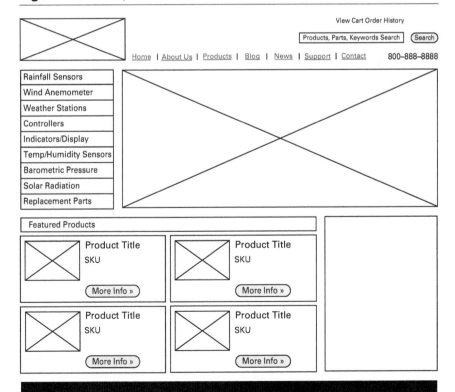

Specialist wireframing tools are available to make it quick and easy to create a wireframe. They come with a number of grids and pre-set shapes and buttons to insert. One of our favourites is Balsamiq but others are widely used including Axure and OmniGraffle. Alternatively, you can always produce a hand-drawn version, or scamp, of the proposed web page.

There are three reasons why it is important that a wireframe is lo-fi and somewhat unfinished-looking:

1 The 'work-in-progress' nature of the wireframe allows everyone to focus on the core experience and functionality of the web page rather than getting distracted by pretty pictures.

2 The wireframe is a device to gather feedback. People are naturally polite and when shown something very highly polished are reluctant to criticize. A line drawing is clearly only work in progress, so reviewers are much more likely to say what they really think.

3 You can expect a lot of changes between the first and the final version of your wireframe. It will be seen by customers and peers, and their feedback incorporated into the final version. It is much quicker and easier simply to create a new wireframe rather than amend polished artwork time and again.

The elements you include in the first version of your wireframe and how you lay them out will be informed by:

- Your research findings
- Device type – it's advisable to make separate wireframes for mobile, tablet and desktop
- New elements you may decide to add in eg new sections, light boxes, pop-ups, etc
- Removal of distracting elements, such as social shares, confusing elements, etc
- Copy requirements – actual words should be shown on the wireframe, in the right hierarchy with more prominence given to important messages. Messages should be carefully placed to guide the viewer to the intended action.

Copy

Copy is an essential part of the wireframe and the exact wording can make a big difference to the impact of a new web page. Often the changes are extremely subtle and the copy may only be a handful of words. We call this 'microcopy', and because it's so short every word counts.

Often the first step is to work out exactly what the requirements of the message are at that particular point, rather than trying to write compelling copy straight off the bat. Is the purpose to educate the visitor? Help them find their way around? Clarify a complex point? Persuade them to take an action?

Use the early stage of the wireframe to work out where to put headlines and sub-heads to make the text scannable.

Once you are clear about what the copy needs to convey, you can rewrite it using copywriting techniques to give it the best chance of achieving the aims set for it.

Among the most valuable techniques are:

- Starting with an active word such as 'Discover' or 'Enjoy' rather than passive words like 'this' or 'A' or 'That'.

- Cutting out unnecessary words.

- Embedded commands such as 'You want that drink to be cold and refreshing'.

- Write in the present continuous tense 'a luminous teapot adds fun and colour to your kitchen' rather than future tense 'a luminous teapot will add fun and colour to your kitchen'. Banish the word 'will'. This technique works because it communicates directly with the sub-conscious brain. Phrased as if something is actually happening right now, the reader imagines themselves using the product or pictures it in their home and feels they must have it.

- Speak directly to the reader, by using words like 'you' and 'your', rather than writing passively in the third person, with phrases like 'We've worked hard'.

- Change company-focused messages (like 'Our biggest ever range') into customer-benefit statements (like 'Your biggest ever choice').

- Assume the sale. Write as if it's tacitly agreed that they are going to buy the product, and talk about 'when you have luminous teapots in your home' rather than 'if you buy the luminous teapots'.

Here are some examples of where a few tiny changes to the message resulted in much more powerful copy – even if at first glance they seem almost identical.

Table 8.1 Examples of powerful copy changes

Original message	New copy	Why?
Seven Days Freshness Guaranteed	Guaranteed Freshness for seven days or more	The word 'guaranteed' hooks the reader, and seven days is support for it. Leading with 'seven' has no meaning until the context is established.
Choose Your Special Offers	You qualify for these special offers:	At this point in the journey, the customer was not aware they would be given an upsell. Copy had to introduce the concept. Starting with the word 'You' helps to hook the eye – everyone is interested in themselves!
Return within two days from delivery date for a full refund	Returns are easy – immediate no-quibble guarantee	At the point of order, people are anxious. Reassuring them that their decision can be reversed reduces risk so increases propensity to go through with the purchase. A surprisingly high number of delivery and returns copy is written in a legalistic-sounding style that can really deter customers from ordering.

Some other tips to bear in mind when developing a wireframe and copy:

- Focus on the visitor behaviour you want to influence – making the wireframe too detailed at this stage will just cost you time
- Use actual copy – not 'lorem ipsum' (filler text) so that you and your reviewers can see how the words are contributing to the change in visitor behaviour that you want to test
- Produce separate wireframes and copy for different device types – their needs, and therefore the creative execution, will be different
- It may be tempting to load it with tactical elements, such as guarantee badges, USP statements and testimonials. However, if everything 'shouts,' nothing is heard. Simplicity is often better. Stick with the plan and focus on your hypothesis.

Step Two: Reviewing the wireframe and copy

It is in the nature of creative work that there could be more than one viable creative solution. That is why it can be useful to get feedback before launching the test, especially from team members who understand the CRO process.

Some CRO practitioners also invite open feedback from the people who took part in earlier usability testing. However, we have found this has limited value because people can't predict their own behaviour. Whenever we open it up to customers, we don't ask them if it works. Instead we ask usability questions such as 'Where would you click?' and 'What would you expect to happen if...?' and so on.

The reviewers can challenge your thinking, spot gaps and generally act as a control to make sure that the solution you are proposing in the wireframe genuinely solves the problem. They may also come up with other creative solutions, even better than the one you thought of.

Your role in the review process is to coordinate all the feedback from your colleagues and customers to determine how your first version of the wireframe and copy can be improved, before it proceeds to artwork.

An easy way to collect and coordinate comments is to use a collaborative notice-board-type application, such as Notable, Realtime Board or Invision. You upload an image of the wireframe together with a description of the changes you have made. State whether it is a new test or an iteration of a previous one and, if so, what the findings were. You also should include key information such as the background to the problem that the wireframe hopes to address, including relevant findings from the qualitative and quantitative data such as:

- the drop-off rate at this point in the journey
- per cent of total visitors to this page
- findings from click maps, heat maps and scroll maps and what this indicates about customer behaviour
- segmented view of behaviour on this page (eg new vs returning visitors)
- comments from usability testers
- snippets from survey responses
- quotes from interviews with customer-facing staff such as live chat or customer service
- goal of test (eg to increase RPV)

There are no set rules – you simply need to give your reviewers enough background to be able to make informed comments. What you choose to tell them depends on the hypothesis and what is to be tested.

You then invite commentators to log in and click on an area of the wireframe to add notes and questions. Everyone sees the other comments and it is possible to reply so you can see the dialogue developing. It is a great way to avoid duplication if several people make the same comment – and have transparency. This also allows you to keep an audit trail of how your first version was influenced by your collaborators' comments.

When you have a well-oiled process in place, your collaborators will know what is expected. However, if you are doing this for the first time, you may want to send out some instructions with your invitation, so that they know what you want from them. Wording like the one below can be helpful and manages expectations, as it may not be possible to use everybody's ideas in the final wireframe.

Dear <collaborator's name>

I have discovered a number of problems that our web visitors are having and would like your help with a proposed new web page.

Please could you give me your feedback and ideas. Just log on to <noticeboard application> to view it and add your comments.

At this stage, it is just a basic version of the new page and some copy. Don't hold back – feel free to be as critical as you like – it will help me enormously. Here are some things to bear in mind when you give your feedback:

- Be specific and tell me exactly how you think could this page be improved

- Offer suggestions as well as criticisms

- Explain the reasons behind your suggestions

- Think about situations where the proposed approach might not work eg out of stock item

- Spot missing information

- Let me know if you have some data that might affect this (I may not have it)

- Ask for clarification if anything is not clear

- Reply to requests for clarification if your comments have not been clearly understood

You can also add drawings and links if that helps. Thanks for your time and the suggestions you may make.

You can also use tools to evaluate and improve your wireframe. Predictive attention mapping tools, such as EyeQuant and Feng-Gui, use an algorithm powered by thousands of previous eye-tracking studies, to predict what the human eye will and, most importantly, won't notice. Use them to ensure that visitors' eyes will be drawn to the most relevant part of the proposed wireframe.

Use the comments you receive on the wireframe, as well as the analysis you gather from tools like EyeQuant to inform and inspire your current thinking and generate further ideas. Remember, though, that you do not have to incorporate everything that is suggested. The single controlling intelligence who has done the research, developed the hypothesis and knows what the website has to achieve, is best placed to bring everything together. Incorporate comments you find useful into the final version and ignore any you do not.

Step Three: Handing over to the development team

Generally, a graphic designer is not required for split test variations. The wireframes are normally handed over to be implemented by the development team on the split testing platform. In technical terms, they use existing Cascading Style Sheets (CSS) so that the variations look part of the existing website.

The technical briefing process to your development team is simple. The wireframe and copy and original web page or pages act as a guide for the developer to make the necessary JavaScript changes. It is important to stress to the developer that they must develop the split test variation exactly as specified in the approved wireframe.

In handing over the wireframe and copy remember to provide your developers with the following information:

- A description of the changes that are to be made, with reference to the wireframe(s)
- An outline of the hypothesis (ie why the changes are being made)
- Any corporate design guidelines such as fonts, grids or colours
- The pages where changes are to be made with the URL(s)
- Goals, which are the metrics to be tracked
- Type of device targeted (eg mobile)
- Segment targeted (eg new visitors only)
- Traffic allocation (eg a 50:50 split)

- Any known browser issues that are likely to have an impact on correct rendering of the variation

- An explanation (or use-case) of new functionality (eg pop-ups, change in data logic, scraping data from other parts of the site)

- How exceptions will be handled (eg what happens if the product is out of stock)

The final stage is for your developers to send you a link to a preview, for you to check that the variation looks and operates exactly as intended. Once the split test is live the exciting part begins as you get to see how your hypothesis and creative execution is received by your website visitors.

Step Four: Optional artwork stage and review stage

The only time you would need a design stage is if you need a new element to be designed, or if a complete re-design is being tested, which is rare. When you do, pick your designer carefully. Normally creativity is a valued quality in a designer but that's the last thing you need in CRO. You need a designer who can work to a tight brief, keeping to brand guidelines and respecting the hierarchy of elements on the page and how they work together to lead the user through the journey. Preferably, they also understand web optimization, both how to create compelling, high converting designs and how to design a page so that it fits seamlessly with the website as a whole.

Some optimization practitioners choose to get feedback on artwork from peers and customers as well as, or instead of, a wireframe. However, this is not necessary or even practical. If we feel we need additional insight, we find it more useful to use predictive attention-mapping tools.

Webpage reviews such as FiveSecondTest, or panel-based usability testing platforms such as WhatUsersDo and UserTesting.com can also reveal issues with your proposed experiment before you make it a live test.

Case study – Xero Shoes

Xero Shoes are unique lightweight and low-profile running sandals. Wearing them is almost like being barefoot. From our research, we knew that customers loved the barefoot feeling, together with having just enough protection against dirt and thorns. The main pre-purchase concern was how comfortable these shoes were, though many reviews raved about comfort.

Figure 8.2 Use of predictive attention mapping tool to compare proposed variation with current page or 'control'

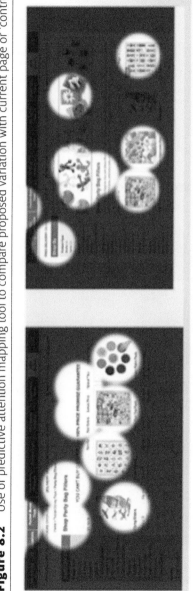

Variant

Control

SOURCE Image courtesy of EyeQuant

Figure 8.3   The wireframe we created for the homepage of Xero Shoes shows the position of images, video and copy

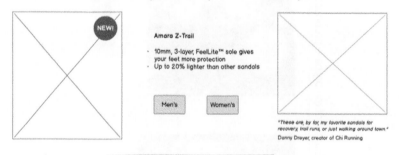

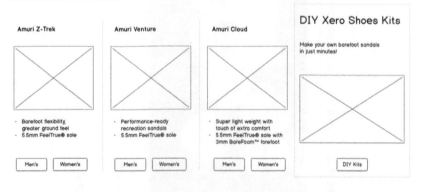

SOURCE Image courtesy of Xero Shoes

Figure 8.4 The actual web page that was tested and resulted in a 6.45 per cent increase in RPV

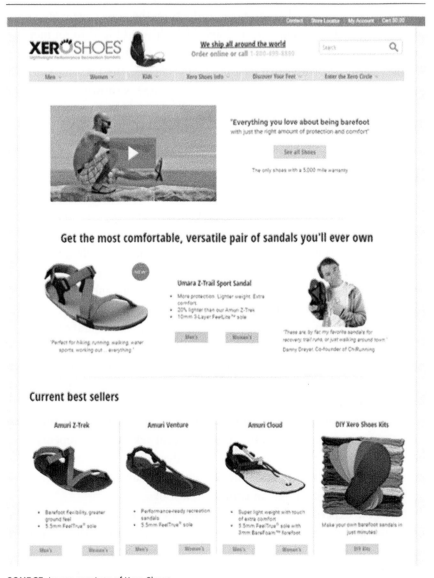

SOURCE Image courtesy of Xero Shoes

When we started working with Xero Shoes, they had no product links on the homepage. The top half of the page was dominated by inspirational images that appealed to their target market. Our research showed us that it was difficult for visitors to form an overall view of the various shoes on offer or the differences between them. Visitors would sometimes return to the homepage to orientate themselves but the only way to find the relevant information was to visit each product page separately.

Our hypothesis was that showing products on the homepage would send more traffic to the Product Detail Pages, which would lead to an increase in sales. We wanted to infuse the page with value statements that we knew would appeal to prospective customers, like Harry, the persona you met in Chapter 4 (Figure 4.1). The resultant wireframe is shown in Figure 8.3 together with the finished page, which yielded a 6.45 per cent increase in Revenue Per Visitor.

Summary

Hypotheses are the building blocks of Conversion Rate Optimization, so the stronger they are, the better the results you obtain in the long run.

The hypothesis is tested in a controlled experiment, usually an A/B test. A positive uplift, in which the new experience performs better than the existing one, validates the hypothesis. When the opposite happens and there is a negative uplift, it is an opportunity to learn more about what customers really need, and develop alternative hypotheses to get the desired behavioural change.

A strong hypothesis statement is more than just a prediction. It includes relevant observations from data, research and analysis, insights gained from these about the issues customers are facing and suggestions for creative solutions to address it.

These suggestions are mapped out in a wireframe, which is subjected to peer review and, occasionally, customer feedback. After comments have been incorporated, the wireframe is given to developers to create a web page in a visual style that melds seamlessly with the main site. Occasionally a graphic designer will design an entirely new look.

This new experience is then split tested by showing some visitors the new page and some the old. After a given period of time, the results are compared to measure the effect of the changes introduced by the variation. At this point, a well-crafted hypothesis helps you to distil valuable insights from the outcome of the experiment, whether positive or negative.

Note

1 Sullivan, C (2015) Myths, Lies and Illusions of AB and Split Testing, LinkedIn Slideshare, slide 36: http://www.slideshare.net/sullivac/myths-lies-and-illusions-of-ab-and-split-testing [accessed 1 July 2016].

Testing your hypotheses 09

Take a wander round Google's offices and before long you'll probably hear their unofficial mantra: 'Data beats opinion'.[1] Split testing is the ultimate business decision-making mechanism because it's driven by the evidence of data.

You're on to a hiding to nothing if you try and ask people how they would behave in a hypothetical scenario. They simply can't predict their own behaviour. It's always more truthful to put them in a situation to measure their behaviour. And that's exactly what split testing does.

The case for split testing

Split testing can help you grow your online business. You can make rational business decisions underpinned by the weight and certainty of data. When do you normally get to make a business decision with 95 per cent confidence that it will give you a good result?

Yet, despite the clear benefits of testing, some business executives and owners are reluctant to split test. You may have some convincing to do to overcome their misplaced beliefs, such as the split testing myths below:

Split Testing Myth 1: 'Most split test results are negative so you lose money'

Okay, it's true that many split tests don't beat the existing website. In fact, on average, only about 40 per cent of tests actually win, according to Experiment Engine.[2] When you're starting out, you could have even fewer wins.

But it's not true to say that business stands to lose money from negative tests. You can refute this with basic maths. There's always a time limit on a split test, so any decline in sales attributable to it will be short-lived. By contrast, every win keeps on adding revenue for months or years after the split test, far outweighing any losses.

An illustration. To keep things simple, let's say that over a period of 10 months, you run 10 split tests, one a month. Six turn out to be negative, down on the control by £1,000 each. You're out of pocket by £6,000 in lost sales.

Imagine if you'd made those six changes live on the site permanently, letting 100 per cent of visitors see them. (A surprising number of companies do that, based on nothing more than liking the way it looks.)

In that scenario, you would have lost £6,000 every month until you somehow realized those changes weren't working as well as before. You'd then get rid of them and be back to square one, with no clue on what to do next. Instead, testing ensured your loss was capped at £6,000 and gave you a wealth of knowledge on how to turn more visitors into customers.

The remaining four tests give you a healthy £1,000 of extra sales each, making a total of £4,000 during the test period. Unlike the tests where sales went down, these you'll keep on running. Over the next year, those four winning tests will continue to bring you in that extra £4,000 every month. That's £48,000 over the course of a year. Take away the £6,000 for the negative tests, and you're still up £42,000 in the first 12 months alone.

But consider this too. Without running those six negative tests, you would never have got to the four winning ones. Negative tests come with the territory. You can't have the one and not the other.

Besides, as Warren Buffet says, 'Some you win, some you learn'. It's the learnings from the tests that don't perform as you would like that let you crack the puzzle and lead you to the meteoric uplifts.

Split Testing Myth 2: 'Other priorities are more urgent'

Some managers like the idea of split testing but let other priorities come first. Replatforming, bug fixing and addressing operational issues are the ones we most commonly hear about.

Of course these need to be dealt with, but it's a question of deciding what's important and what's urgent. Whatever the reasons for delaying split testing, the impact is the same – losing valuable time and falling further behind the competition. Talk about leaving money on the table!

It's actually an argument for bumping split testing higher up the agenda. It can give you vital insights that could inform those very initiatives that are causing the delay.

Split Testing Myth 3: 'It's too expensive'

Saying that split testing is too dear is like saying that you can't afford to do any marketing. What else should you be investing your money in, if not activities to help you generate more money from the same amount of expenditure?

When you consider the cost of the lost opportunities, then it's really the absence of split testing that's expensive.

Split Testing Myth 4: 'It wastes time'

E-commerce managers want results quickly but unfortunately split tests take time to run. However, it's a false economy to view this as slowing down the business. As long as you put a ceiling on test duration, as discussed later, split testing won't hold you back and your developers will only implement changes on the site that have proved their worth.

Split Testing Myth 5: 'We want to invest in getting more traffic first'

A bit of a chicken and egg situation, as you can't improve conversion rates if there aren't any visitors to convert. But if you already have an existing flow of traffic, why not tune up your site so that more of the visitors you already have will turn into customers and actually spend money when they get there.

Shelling out to shovel ever greater numbers of visitors into a site that doesn't convert is like scattering ever bigger sacks of seed onto barren land. If you want a bumper harvest, get the soil fertile first.

Split Test Myth 6: 'We don't have enough traffic'

It's true that if your site is small it can be a challenge to run tests that are statistically significant. However, it may still be possible. In some ways split testing is even more important for a small site because it really does have to focus on extracting value from its few visitors. More on this topic later.

Split Test Myth 7: 'Our technology is too unstable'

You'd like to split test but you're concerned that your ancient platform is too rickety. Don't let it get in the way of making improvements to your site that can potentially fund the required upgrade. By delaying it, you're being left further and further behind. When you finally get around to updating the old technology, it won't magically optimize the site for buying.

Split Test Myth 8: 'You can never trust the results of a split test'

It's true that if you break the rules, split test results are not to be trusted. However, if you follow basic principles outlined in this chapter, ensure you have a decent sample size and run the test for long enough, you'll have results you can rely on.

Types of split test

Split testing is an umbrella term that covers mainly two different types:

A/B testing
Multivariate testing (MVT)

The type you use will depend on what you want to find out about your visitors and where you are in your optimization programme.

Whichever test you use, though, remember that even if you hope to get a win, the outcome you plan for is to get a learning. Every test has a value if you can learn something from it. As Thomas Edison, the famous light bulb inventor, said when he was questioned about all his failures: 'I have not failed. I've just found 10,000 ways that won't work.'

A/B test

This is the staple of the industry and most of your tests will fall into this category. It's simply comparing one variation against the control, where 50 per cent of the audience see Version A (the original web page, also known as the control) and the rest see a new variation, Version B (your variation, sometimes called the challenger). If there is more than one variation, it is known as an A/B/*n* test.

As you will have seen from the previous chapters, there are endless things that you can A/B test, such as:

- Changing a single element such as a headline, image or delivery cost messaging
- A new structure

- A radical redesign of a page
- A redirect, where the variation being tested is a different URL or flow
- Complete web experience involving more than one page, eg a different checkout sequence. (This is sometimes called a multipage test)
- A personalized experience versus a non-personalized one

Multivariate test (MVT)

With MVT, you test the control against a number of variables, dynamically arranged into different combinations. Let's say you want to find the best headline and hero image combination. You can load alternative headlines and images into the testing tool and it will mock up all possible combinations on the fly.

One major drawback of MVT is that it demands exponentially more traffic than a straightforward A/B/n test. Frankly, this puts it out of reach of most websites. If you do have enough traffic to warrant MVT, the number one benefit is accelerated learning. It's a great way of pointing out the most profitable levers on a page or on your site.

Our recommendation is to use MVT only to identify those elements, then to target these with A/B testing but don't use it at all unless you have lots of traffic.

Exclusion test

This can be either A/B/n or MVT. Sometimes called an existence test, it helps you determine and quantify the effect of a given page element. The basic idea is to hide that component in your variation to see what difference it makes.

You may encounter resistance to this idea, chiefly because it goes against the grain for some people to remove an existing element from a page. But the fact is that, in certain situations, it will give you hard data to back up decisions you know will need to be made.

If the experiment shows an uplift, it serves as an indication that the particular variable may be damaging to sales. The results can be surprising, even counter-intuitive. Should that happen, think carefully through the possibilities of why that could be and what it tells you about your customer preferences.

If the test gives you a negative uplift, it's an indication that the element you hid in the test does make a difference to sales. Of course you should leave it in, but can you do more with it? If results are inconclusive, it could be a sign that the element can work harder for you or, conversely, that the space it takes up can be put to better use.

Here's an interesting example. It's a truism that money back guarantees and friendly returns policies give people the reassurance they need to buy, so they bump up sales. And most of the time that's what happens.

So it was a surprise when we took a guarantee off the website of one of our clients and saw an increase in revenue. Why? The site sold gifts for children. When we investigated we found out that many sales were grandparents buying for their grandchildren. The last thing a grandfather wants to contemplate when buying a gift for his grandson is that things will go wrong and, heaven forbid, the gift has to be returned. The money-back guarantee planted a seed of doubt.

With this type of experiment, always test only one variable at a time so that you can isolate the value of that particular thing being tested. If you want to test more than one element, then run separate variations (A/B/n formulation) or do sequential tests.

Big and small changes

Debate rages in CRO circles as to whether it is better to test big bold radical changes or small alterations. Strong cases are made by both camps.

The philosophy behind incremental testing is that you're continuously making little changes, banking small uplifts all the way. See Figure 9.1 for an example, a small change tested on the homepage of the Cox & Cox mobile site. In the control, on the left, each category is represented by an image. Our variation, on the right, removed the images and simply replaced it with tabs. It was 17 per cent more effective in sending traffic to PDPs, which is a key objective of the homepage, and led to an increase in revenue of 6 per cent.

All those 'almost nothings' eventually amount to something. The problem is that small changes often lack the muscle to deliver any noticeable effect, yielding inconclusive results. This wastes weeks of testing time and inconclusive results mean it's hard to draw meaningful insights.

Radical changes such as a complete redesign of a page are more likely to bring about a significant difference in behaviour and, therefore, cause a more noticeable effect, either positive or negative. However, when you have more than one variable in an experiment, you can't be sure which ones are working in your favour and which ones are pulling the overall result down. The more you have, the more difficult it becomes to pinpoint cause and effect.

Figure 9.1 An example of an incremental test, conducted on the mobile site of Cox & Cox, showing the control on the left and the variant on the right

SOURCE Image courtesy of Cox & Cox

Radical changes demand more time for hypothesizing, wireframing and coding. If it delivers a positive uplift, the investment pays off. If it bombs out, not only do you not have an uplift, but it's also more difficult to learn from it. The CRO workflow platform Experiment Engine found that only 16 per cent of big uplifts came from radical testing.[3]

It's a trade-off between potential impact (radical) versus more precise learning (incremental). Our view is that the right approach is a balance between the two.

Making the choice

What makes it tricky is that 'radical' is a matter of perspective and therefore open to interpretation. Our advice is to stick primarily to experiments that allow you to learn. We define radical tests as ones where there are so many factors that it's hard to draw conclusions, or ones that would take a long time to develop. Any test that lends itself to iterative learning in a reasonable amount of time, regardless of how many variables are changed, goes in the 'incremental testing' budget in our view.

With incremental testing, you can create layers of insight with every iteration, that gradually build up to a big win. Daniel Lee, Web Analyst of UK's leading cycle retailer, Evan Cycles, talks about 'getting close to your superior point of optimization, and then iterating around this point.'[4] You find your optimal position in the grid (Figure 9.2) by incrementally testing towards each area.[5] For example, in Chapter 5 we advised discovering your value proposition by testing different themes against each other. In this illustration, visitors react better to the Price Guarantee than to the other value claims. The oval represents the area where you would iterate around this winning theme. Future experiments might iteratively test different attributes of the same theme eg location on the page or in the funnel, messaging and creative.

No need to wait until you start with small scale incremental testing. The research and analysis phase is the perfect time for it, because your purpose is accelerating insights generation. The Optimization Plan is not ready yet, so there's no risk of hijacking valuable testing slots.

If you favour incremental testing and find that a lot of your experiments are inconclusive or do not make noticeable impact, it's definitely time to be bolder.

If the design or structure of the current template is too limiting for the changes that you want to make, this is also a clear sign that you need to take a more radical approach. Equally, if you reach a point of diminishing returns

Figure 9.2   Strategic theme exploration

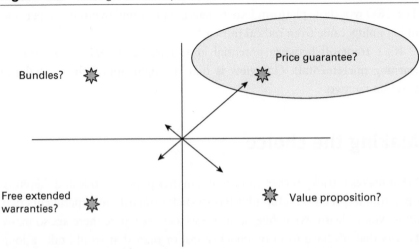

SOURCE Adapted from Daniel Lee

Figure 9.3 Local and global maxima

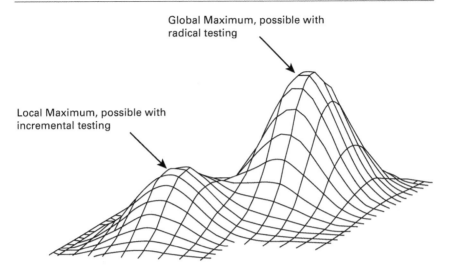

Global Maximum, possible with
radical testing

Local Maximum, possible with
incremental testing

after making incremental gains at first, it's time to go bolder. Once you've found a new template that works, you can continue optimizing it with incremental testing. It is known as the 'local maximum'. This means that relative to the tests you have been running you have reached the maximum, but not relative to all the potential gains if you started from a different base. It's like climbing up the small hill in Figure 9.3, whereas in fact there's a much higher hill a short distance away.

Statistics for optimizers

When you interpret split test results, you are making inferences about your entire audience based on what you've observed from a sample. How confident can you really be about those extrapolations? Are you guaranteed to see the same revenue uplifts once the web page goes live on the site? In fact, some statisticians believe that nearly all winning split test results are actually illusory.[6]

You want to try and avoid those tests that look exciting but fail to make a real difference. The best way to improve your chances of picking the real winners is to gain an understanding of the relevant statistical principles. Detailed technical explanations are beyond the scope of this book but some of the key concepts are explained below in simple terms, to give you a working knowledge that will stand you in good stead.

Figure 9.4 A dashboard of Qubit's Digital Experience Platform shows Statistical Power prominently, top left. Even though there is a high (99.86 per cent) probability of a strong lift, the experiment has to collect more data before we can be confident that this effect really exists

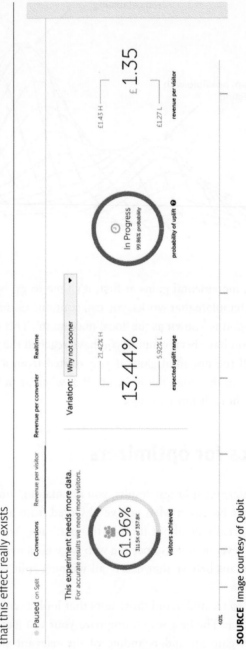

SOURCE Image courtesy of Qubit

Statistical significance

This tells us whether there really is a meaningful difference between the control and variation. As a general rule, we look for a statistical significance level of 95 per cent. That sounds reassuring, but what it means is that there is a 5 per cent chance of it being a fluke. So, one out of 20 'confident' wins is false.

Statistical significance is used by many as a comfort blanket but there are dangers in relying on this alone. To be sure your test is worth putting live, you should look at the other factors below.

Statistical power

Optimizely describes statistical power as 'a measure of whether your test has adequate data to reach a conclusive result'.[7] It comes down to having a large enough sample for us to detect an effect if it really exists.

Technically, it's possible to improve the power of a test in a number of ways. Practically, the most within your control is increasing the sample size, in other words letting more visitors into the test, usually by running it for longer. Another way would be to try for a bigger effect, which refers to the magnitude of difference between the control and variation. For more on this, see the section on Minimum Detectable Effect below.

An under-powered test holds the risk of either overlooking a true winner, or declaring a confident winner which doesn't really exist. A statistical power value of 0.80 is industry standard, used across research fields. This means there's a reasonable chance (80 per cent) of detecting a given effect if it exists.

Minimum Detectable Effect (MDE)

As the name suggests, this is the minimum lift that you want the tool to detect. If a lift is detected below the MDE threshold, you won't know about it. Why would you want to potentially miss smaller effects? Because, below the MDE, it won't reach statistical significance with the sample size available to you. The only way to increase the sample size, so as to reach statistical significance, would be to increase test duration. The lower the MDE, the longer your test will have to run. So the MDE lets you weed out tests that will take too long to mature, given your traffic levels. It lets you make best use of your time and helps you keep the momentum.

How should you determine the MDE? You can't predict the outcome of a test, otherwise you wouldn't be running it in the first place! The key is to

Figure 9.5 A screenshot from a test result in Optimizely, illustrating regression to mean. This is a common pattern, so be careful of jumping to conclusions before the test has run its course

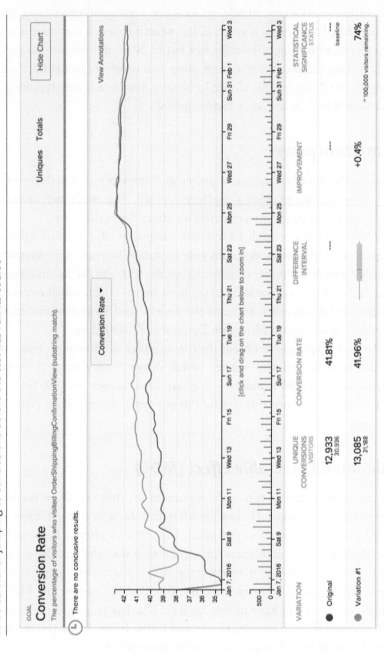

SOURCE Image courtesy of Optimizely

set a level that is *meaningful*[8] and *practical*.[9] Waiting months for a winning result to be declared is not practical, so that argues in favour of increasing the MDE. What is a meaningful lift? Is 1 per cent good? Not if you're a small business, but if you're turning over millions of pounds, then it could make a difference. Many platforms now employ statistics engines which remove the requirement to determine sample size and MDE in advance. Check your vendor documentation.

Confidence intervals

A reported uplift of say 10 per cent doesn't mean that the win is locked in at exactly 10 per cent. There is a range within which that number can fluctuate at levels of 95 per cent statistical significance; it could be higher or lower. This range of possible values is known as the confidence interval. The longer you run a test, the smaller this range becomes. In Figure 9.4 above, you can see that the test has a reported RPV of £1.35. It is flanked by values of £1.27 and £1.43, representing the lower and upper limits of the confidence interval at that point in time.

Regression to the mean

Below is a typical report for an experiment from Optimizely, one of the leading split testing platforms. The graph shows RPV for the control and your variation, which contains the changes. The top line is the variation and the bottom line is the control.

In this example, it starts off looking promising for the variation. But after two weeks it's lost all that initial shine. Even then, it's tempting to remain hopeful about the prospect of a win. Indeed, it's possible that some external variable could have had an impact. However, the more plausible explanation is that there never was any real difference between the two. What we observed initially were fluctuations which normalized over time as the coin was flipped more times. This is known as regression to mean.

How long should a split test run?

There is a minimum required sample size for every test you run. It's a complex subject, which cannot be reduced to well-meaning rules of thumb, such as the popular suggestion to observe 100 to 400 conversions per variation.

It depends on a number of variables including the underlying statistical models employed by the testing platform. Most tool providers offer calculators on their websites that will enable you to work out required test duration and/or sample size. Before you implement any test, do take advantage of their calculators to work out the sample size that will serve your needs best.

Furthermore, in our agency, we usually insist on running a test for at least 14 days. Buying behaviour could fluctuate significantly depending on the day of the week, so we want to observe at least two full weeks and weekends.

The purchasing cycle

Longer purchase cycles could mean that certain tests have to be run for longer. Customers don't always make up their mind immediately, especially for higher-priced items. A visitor can enter the test on Day 1 but not purchase until Day 20. Clearly, the conversion will only be counted at that point. If the test ended after 14 days, that conversion would not have been taken into account at all.

Generally speaking, this is not a major issue because the effect will apply to the same extent to the control and variation. However, if a large portion of transactions are likely to be missed by a 14-day window, you should think about accounting for it by extending the run. To get a steer on this, consult the *Time to Purchase* report in GA.

Split testing low traffic sites

Given the importance of sample size when running split tests, you might think that only big websites can benefit from website optimization. However, there are still things you can do if your site is low on traffic. Here are some ideas.

Track micro conversions

Throughout this book, we stress the importance of using Revenue Per Visitor (RPV) as a primary goal. However, if sales activity is low, this could take months, especially if there is a great deal of variance in basket values.

If this applies to you, then Conversion Rate might be a better metric, although even that could take a while if your site generates only a few orders per week. Another option is to track micro conversions such as progression to next page or clicks on the 'add to basket' button. Common sense tells you that when you have more micro conversions you'll have a higher overall conversion rate. Be warned, that doesn't always correlate.

Focus on impact

The greater the effect of the test, the smaller the sample you need. Low-traffic sites should therefore shoot for a bigger impact. As we said earlier, radical testing is more likely to produce pronounced effects than testing small changes. Whether positive or negative, this allows you to move forward quickly.

Use a test duration calculator to work out the uplift you need to target in order to get statistically robust results in a reasonable time frame. Do this by setting different values of Minimum Detectable Effect (MDE), which will give you an idea of how bold you may need to be with your execution.

Remove outliers

Revenue goals require a lot more data than conversion rate to reach conclusion. This is because a conversion is a straightforward binary yes or no, whereas revenue can vary almost infinitely. One basket value could be £10 and the next one £1,000. If there's a great deal of variance in your data, tests will take a lot longer to mature. We've seen instances where just one big purchase has got in the way of things. You could overcome this by exporting the data from your split test, and removing the outliers as part of a manual calculation. A trained data analyst should be able to do this. If you don't have one on your team, consider hiring a freelance statistician or data analyst on Upwork or PeoplePerHour to do the calculation. It shouldn't be more than an hour's work if all the data is ready.

Lower the statistical significance threshold

Some tools allow you to set a lower statistical significance level. Ultimately, it is a decision about the level of risk you're willing to take. Having 80 per cent confidence, rather than 95 per cent confidence, is still better than making a guess if your alternative is not testing at all.

Avoid multiple variations

The more variations you have in your test, the more your traffic has to be split up. If your small sample size has to be split three ways instead of two, you'll need more traffic. Stick to A/B tests – one variation at a time.

Target higher traffic areas

The further you move down the funnel of your customer journey, the lower traffic volume will be. Typically, checkout pages see a fraction of the traffic of a product detail page. The basket page falls somewhere in between.

Balanced against this is the fact that when you're closer to the entrance of the funnel, the lower the purchase conversion rate will be. This tactic therefore forces you to use micro conversion metrics which may not be as helpful as RPV and purchase conversion rate.

How to avoid common testing problems

After all this effort, the last thing you want is for test results to be rendered invalid as a result of technical glitches or for the split test to cause your site to break. Here are some tips that will help you avoid that.

Implement the tool correctly

Duh! But seriously. Make sure that the tool provider's implementation instructions have been followed to the letter. Check that the software is correctly deployed. We've seen things go wrong because the code had not been deposited in exactly the right position on the page. We recommend avoiding placement via a tag management tool.

Do a site code assessment

This highlights atypical pages or inconsistencies in the code on the site which can throw off experiment targeting or triggering. Also ensure that all required JavaScript libraries, and versions of those libraries, exist on the site.

QA your test

Don't make any test live without solid QA (quality assurance). We have often caught issues during QA that could have been detrimental to sales had it gone live. Check that everything is working properly in all major browsers. Go beyond the page targeted by the experiment. For example, if the test runs on the Product Detail Page (PDP), go through the entire process of adding a product to the cart and advancing to the basket page.

Fire up the preview link in whatever browser you have on your machine but don't stop there. Use one of the browser emulators (see Chapter 4 for a list) to fill in the gaps. Do the same for different device types and even different screen sizes, if your test targets multiple devices.

Reduce flicker

Occasionally there may be a brief delay before the variation is visible in the browser. This could mean that the user gets a fleeting glimpse of the original live page, before seeing it change to the variation. Depending on the severity, it can be rather disconcerting. Even more importantly, it can skew your test results.

To prevent this, place the code for the tool on the page exactly as recommended by the vendor. Should you encounter flicker, ask your developers to try one of the following:

Progressive loading: ensure your test code runs as early as possible and have the variation progressively load over the top of the original page. The downside to this is the extra logic needed to poll for various elements, which takes longer and complicates the code.

Blanking: a little-known trick is to add some code to the control as well, which will stop it from loading until the variation is ready. In this way, the variation doesn't get penalized unfairly by a slightly slower page-load speed. This is the easier option, but least preferable since it blanks out the control, even if only by a few milliseconds.

Limit changes during an experiment

Don't make any changes to a test while it's in progress. If you can't avoid it, you should pause it, and then clone to start it afresh. Also avoid making changes to the site code in those areas where experiments are in progress. The variation code could have dependencies on seemingly unimportant elements on a page.

Even small changes like copy could break an entire test. If this isn't practical, you need to build your test code to be as adaptable as possible, so that it can handle small changes. Always preview any changes in User Acceptance Testing (UAT).

Be cautious of parallel experiments

The validity of running multiple experiments at the same time is often debated. There's a strong argument that you should run no more than one experiment at a time, since two or more simultaneous tests can contaminate each other.

You can limit this risk in two ways. Firstly, never run two or more experiments in the same area of the site. So, you may have one targeting the Product Detail Page (PDP) and another in the checkout. If you do that, consider carefully how the one may impact on the other. A more watertight option is to make parallel tests mutually exclusive so that a visitor can only be bucketed into one of them.

Control for seasonal effects

Seasonal effects can cause your customers to behave differently. For example, motivation to buy is generally higher during the run-up to Christmas and over sale periods. Don't shy away from testing in these times. If large portions of your annual revenue are attributable to certain peak periods, you should be optimizing for those. Because of increased traffic it's also possible to get more accurate results faster.

To check for the impact of seasonality, you could run a follow-on test at a later time. You could also leave a stub of the test running by setting the winning variation to 95 per cent of traffic with the remaining 5 per cent still seeing the control. This will show the effect over time, as explained later in this chapter. Clearly, if most of your revenue is generated over those peak periods, it would be unwise to turn off the test in those times.

Should you run an a/a test?

The short answer is no. In an a/a test, there is no difference between the two variations. Essentially, you're testing the page against itself. Some commentators have advised doing it to check for setup issues. The reality is that you're wasting time that should be spent running a real test. If you stick to the other guidelines, there's no need for this.

Interpreting test results

To measure the performance of the variation against the control, the split testing interface will prompt you to select the most relevant metrics to set as goals. Metrics are the measuring sticks for your split tests. It is what enables you to

see how the variation changes behaviour. The right metrics can help you interpret the outcome of a test by asking why behaviour changed in the way it did.

Primary metric

The primary metric should be chosen for its ability to directly measure that
behaviour which the experiment tries to change. This is because you'll use it
to determine whether the hypothesis is validated or rejected.

Definition of website conversion rate

Conversion rate is a measure of how effectively your site converts visitors
into paying customers. It is a default secondary metric in e-commerce split
testing, but is often used as a primary metric if RPV is not possible.
  Conversion rate = transactions/visits

For e-commerce sites, the ideal primary metric is **Revenue Per Visitor (RPV)**.
Why not **Conversion rate**? Because there are times when a high conversion
rate gives you less money. How? Take a look at the two scenarios below.

Scenario A: You have four visitors. One of them places an order for £50 – that's
a 25 per cent conversion rate.

Scenario B: Again you have four visitors, but this time two place an order – that's
a whopping 50 per cent conversion rate. However, each customer only spends
£10. That's £20 in total revenue, less than half of Scenario A.

Which would you rather have – the scenario with 25 per cent conversion
rate or the one with 50 per cent conversion rate? As you can see, conversion
rate can be misleading. You can't bank a higher conversion rate.

Having said that, there are circumstances where RPV won't serve your
purposes. For example, if you don't have enough traffic you may need to
look at conversion rate or other metrics. Cash is king, so always try to get
as close as possible to measuring revenue.

To illustrate, the metrics below all measure revenue-generating activities
on a clothing site but each tier is further removed from revenue.

- Conversion rate
- Item added to cart
- Size/colour selected
- Visits to Product Detail Page

So we recommend that you use RPV as your primary metric as far as possible, making sure that you look at site-wide revenue, not just the percentage revenue uplift reported by your split testing platform. That may not give you the full picture.

For example, if you have a 34 per cent increase in RPV among visitors who have been on your Privacy Policy, but they only make up 2 per cent of all visitors, then in effect you only have a 0.68 per cent increase in site-wide revenue (ie: 2 per cent of 34 per cent). While the 34 per cent uplift may be substantial, the small segment to which this uplift can be applied renders the overall increase rather underwhelming.

Secondary metrics

Important as the primary metric may be, it only gives you one dimension. To squeeze the most insights out of your experiments, you need to build in extra layers of information by tracking secondary metrics. These help you construct a narrative around the outcome of an experiment. For example, if you are running a test around the site's main navigation you may want to consider these secondary metrics.

You'll find that secondary metrics often reach statistical significance before the primary metric. Or it could happen that the primary metric is

Table 9.1   A list of secondary metrics that enable you to build a narrative around an experiment targeting the site's main navigation

Secondary metric	Why it's relevant
Conversion rate (The default secondary metric)	It's closely tied to revenue, and shows how effective the variation is at turning visitors into customers
Clicks on navigation	Shows you to what extent any changes to the menu affected visitor behaviour
Site search activity	Perhaps the menu changes introduced by the variation will cause more visitors to use site search instead
Page views on PLPs (Product Listing Pages)	If the main purpose of the site's navigation is to direct visitors to the PLPs, then let's measure the difference in behaviour from this perspective too

inconclusive, or even negative, while one or more of the secondary metrics reflect a statistically significant uplift.

If that happens, it can be tempting to use a secondary metric to call a win, but you should resist it. Secondary metrics are seldom closely enough linked to the hypothesis to validate or refute it.

Use secondary metrics to explain primary metric performance.

Whatever the performance of the primary metric, secondary metrics can help you to explain the overall result. Ask what each secondary metric tells you about a change in visitor behaviour. Why is it different to, or the same as the primary metric?

Although you can't read too much into any metrics that haven't reached statistical significance, they can boost what you learn from the test to help you get a bigger win next.

Post-test segmentation

Unless the test is configured to target a pre-determined segment exclusively, the result relates to the entire test audience. However, we all know that people are not the same and it's likely that different groups of visitors behave differently. Averages lie. Quite possibly you got a win from one segment, but it got cancelled out by another losing segment.

Most testing platforms offer post-test segmentation, sometimes at additional cost. You can however integrate the split test with GA for free, which we highly recommend. This enables you to do even deeper segmented analysis in GA. These are the type of segments you could look at:

- Desktop vs mobile
- New vs returning visitors
- Traffic source
- Browser or operating system

As you compare the performance of different segments, try to explain any differences in behaviour. Why did particular segments respond as they did? If there's any difference in performance, why would that be?

Don't jump to conclusions based on segmented reporting as it increases your chance of finding a fluke win, or 'false positive' in statistical terms. There will be more random fluctuation due to smaller sample sizes. Also bear in mind that one segment in isolation cannot give you the full picture.

Margin in RPV-based tests

Your accountant will remind you that 'revenue is vanity, profit is sanity'. Sometimes it's vital that you account for margin by bringing underlying cost drivers into the calculation.

For one of our clients, an international fashion brand, we ran a split test that introduced free delivery above a certain basket value. Since the site offered free returns, we thought that some customers might order more than one item to qualify for free delivery, only to return part of the order later.

Having integrated the split test with GA, we were able to export from GA unique *Transaction IDs*. Matching these with the client's back-end data, we pulled in the relevant transaction details. That enabled us to calculate and compare product return rate, as well as subtract return values from the revenue reported by the test. This ensured that we weren't giving the variation an unfair advantage by reporting inflated revenue figures.

Declaring a win

Unfortunately, there's no easy checklist to help you decide whether a win is a sure enough bet to run with it. There are too many variables, plus it requires a level of human interpretation.

At a minimum, check your experiment against these guidelines before declaring a win:

- Has it been seen by the number of visitors recommended by the test duration calculator?
- Has it been running for at least two business cycles, normally 14 days?
- Is there an increase in the primary metric, most commonly Revenue Per Visitor (RPV) of at least 2 per cent?
- Has it achieved statistical significance of at least 95 per cent unless you have agreed to settle on a lower value for good reason?
- If the win relates to a segment, is the sample size large enough to draw conclusions?

Make the winning experience live

Clearly you want to get the benefit of a winning variation as soon as possible. You have three options when it comes to rolling out the changes on your site:

1 Serve the winning variation to 100 per cent of visitors, rather than 50 per cent as before

2 Hard-code the winning variation, to make it a permanent feature of the site

3 Run a stub, where 5 per cent of website visitors continue to see the control

Below is a summary of the pros and cons of each of these approaches.

If you follow the hard-coding route, you can help speed things up greatly by giving your web development team or agency a good brief, covering the following:

● Screenshots of the control and variations

● Outline of differences introduced by the variations

● Any changes to business logic

● Results achieved during the test

● Code created for the variation in the split testing tool's code engine

● Any special events that require additional QA/checking in development

As with any change to your site, review this implementation on your staging server before it goes live. Make sure it's a carbon copy of the winning variation, that it looks and functions exactly the same. It sounds like an obvious thing, but we have seen this be ignored once too often.

External validation of results

Your boss wants to validate a winning experiment by looking for 'proof' in GA or back-end sales data. Or the Finance Director wants to integrate uplifts neatly into their budgets. Be warned – it's not that straightforward.

Firstly, the effects of most experiments will be drowned in the default aggregate numbers, where most people may be scratching around. This is because it targets only a small area of the total site, and therefore you have to consider site-wide revenue as we explained earlier. On top of that, the winning variation was only seen by 50 per cent of that segment, so you can't expect the full effect to be noticeable in the aggregate.

Secondly, you can't account for external hidden variables like seasonality, traffic mix, sale periods and bugs. Imagine that, on the day you make a strong winner live, your company gets unexpected media coverage. Suddenly, there's an influx of site visitors who are overwhelmingly curious, tyre kickers. Of course, this will affect your overall conversion rate negatively as there are more visitors for the same number of buyers. Forget the idea of before and after comparison.

Table 9.2 Options to integrate a positive split test result into the live site

#	Criteria	Advantages	Disadvantages	Recommendation
1	Split testing platform serves winning variation to 100% of website visitors	All visitors will see the winning variation, and instead of getting only 50% of the uplift, you get all of it. It is quick and easy; you save development costs in the short term	If the page targeted by the experiment is updated often, then serving the winning variation over extended periods of time may negatively impact the website's operation	Use this approach only in the short term, for example if your development team have a backlog
			If updates are made to your website platform, the winning variation can 'break' and no longer work as before	
			Generally speaking and with the exception of personalization tools, split testing platforms are not built to be serving winning variations on a continuous basis	
			At the time of writing, Google's guidelines on split testing state that you should only serve variations as long as is necessary, in other words until the experiment is concluded[1]	

2	Hard-code the winning variation	The winning variation becomes part of the permanent code of the website. If implemented and tested correctly this will be the most reliable option	Integrating this version into the website's code will require development resource, and there may be a backlog	If you have development resource available this is the most sensible option
3	Serve the winning variation to 95% of the audience, and let 5% of them still see the control	You can validate the win on an ongoing basis, and check for seasonal and perishability effects. Perishability is when an uplift gradually fades out, which can happen for many reasons This option will be useful if you're likely to need external validation at a later time	If regular changes are made to your website, this could cause the variation to 'break'	This is the right option if you have treated a relatively static part of the website and want to see what uplift the winning variation continues to produce on an ongoing basis

¹ Moskwa, S (2012) *Website testing & Google search*, available from: https://googlewebmastercentral.blogspot.co.uk/2012/08/website-testing-google-search.html (accessed: 1 July 2016)

The good news is that there is a way to validate results externally by integrating the split test with GA. It lets you cut out the noise of aggregate data, drilling down into segments where you can compare the effect of the variation against the control. Another good way of external validation is by running a 5 per cent stub of the control, as explained in Table 9.2 above.

How to deal with negative tests

As we've seen, the majority of split tests fail to produce an uplift. That doesn't mean they are failures though. There are no 'losing' tests. Though we tend to refer to lifts as 'wins', the opposite is by no means a 'loss' – provided you follow a structured approach. Practitioners call them 'negative uplifts', which may sound oxymoronic, so let's look at the upside of a negative result:

Done properly, you will learn something valuable about visitor behaviour or customer preference. Not only can this knowledge save you money in the long run, but negative tests often prompt iterations that produce positive lifts larger than the initial loss. In fact, some of our most impressive results were for what we call 'turnaround tests'. This is when the first run is negative but subsequent iterations deliver positive results thanks to the insights drawn from the initial negative.

The initial negative result should therefore be seen as an investment with a positive ROI. Optimization is not about short-term gains. Far more important is learning about what works and what doesn't. That intelligence will pay healthy dividends over time. Of course wins are important but if that's your primary focus, you won't enjoy the full benefit of testing.

In fact, it's a good habit to consider what you will learn from a negative result in advance, at the point where you create your test hypothesis. Ask: 'What will I learn if this is negative?' If you can't answer this question, consider tweaking the test so that it's a win-win situation, regardless of the outcome.

What to do when you have a negative test

Look for answers in the secondary metrics. In this way, you can construct a narrative of how the test changed user behaviour. Recently, we put a product finder wizard on a client's homepage, which led to a negative impact on RPV. The secondary metrics enabled us to piece together what had happened. A lot of people interacted with the wizard, which didn't surprise us given its prominence. However, this took them out of the default path of discovery and inspiration, which is quite important on this particular site. It helped us understand where to focus our efforts in future.

Post-test segmentation is always important, but especially so in the case of a negative uplift. What does it tell you about preference or behavioural differences between the various user groups? Again, insights come from asking why those segments performed differently. Record the learning, as you would do for any other test. As we said before, be wary of 'hidden winners' found in segments. Rather set up a follow-on test targeting that winning segment specifically to validate the finding.

Make adjustments and retest. If the experiment was based on a data-driven hypothesis as it should be, the underlying observations remain unchanged. It's possible you just haven't found the right way of responding to it. Only when you have a series of negative iterations will you realize that this may be a signal that the opportunity had been overestimated. If that should happen, document the insights and move on.

CASE STUDY

Thompson & Morgan

Thompson & Morgan is a brand leader in plants, seeds and fruit trees. Customers love Thompson & Morgan for its wide variety of merchandise and many of them spend hours browsing the site. We found that shoppers were heavily influenced by images.

Product listing pages (PLPs) are a vital part of how they discover Thompson & Morgan's full range of merchandise. We hypothesized that showing more products on the PLP, and using larger images, would better show off the breadth of offering, and would improve the buying experience. This meant changing the PLP from a list view to a grid layout.

The experiment was negative. As to why this could have been the case, we identified a few possibilities:

- The hypothesis that more and larger images on the PLP would improve the buying experience was incorrect.
- Basic product information, which was present in the list view but removed from the grid view, is vital for customers to make their purchase decision.
- Showing the breadth of offering actually made it more difficult to make a choice, a concept known as the 'paradox of choice'.

Each of these possible explanations gives rise to new ideas, so it led to a few more experiments in this area. We found that larger images were in fact better, but showing basic product information at this point in the journey was equally important. That was the insight that we needed to have in order to generate decent wins on this page. The only way to get to this learning was by testing it, and working with the negative result.

How to deal with inconclusive tests

An inconclusive result is when there is no statistically significant difference, whether up or down, between the control and your variation. If you're seeing many inconclusive results, this may be a sign that you aren't being brave enough. Bolder tests should move the dial more strongly either way. It could also imply that hypotheses are not well structured, or that badly researched ideas are slipping through.

Generally, handle it the same as negative tests. Ask why it made no difference. Why did the change not manage to influence users to behave in a different way? What can be read into that? Document the insight. Conduct post-test segmentation and consider why different segments respond in the way they do. Adjust the test execution, and run another experiment to treat the same hypothesis. Or adjust the hypothesis before retesting.

Document test results

Diligent documentation goes hand in hand with split testing. A test is not done until everything has been recorded. You also need to loop it back into your Optimization Plan so you can build on the learnings. Give each test a unique name, used as a unique identifier in all documentation.

Knowledge base

Set up a knowledge base where results and insights can be captured. This is a detailed record of every split test. It doesn't have to be fancy. A spreadsheet in the cloud is all you need, but you may want to consider using one of the bespoke CRO management tools listed in Chapter 7. It is an inventory of experiments, detailing the tests that were run, with timings and results as well as notes on hypotheses, insights and conclusions. It quickly becomes a huge institutional asset with benefits way beyond website optimization.

After each split test result, update your knowledge base in the following areas:

- Unique ID
- Descriptive title
- Type of test
- Number of variations

- Audience or segments targeted
- Number of visitors per variation
- Hypothesis
- Area of website treated
- Source(s) of insight
- Start and end date of test
- Cost to create and run split test
- Cost to implement split test (if hard-coded)
- Screenshots of the control and variations
- Outline of the changes introduced
- Primary metric and uplift
- Statistical significance
- Annualized revenue impact on the business
- Key segments
- Key learnings
- Next steps

Test conclusion report

The knowledge base also serves as the basis of what goes out to stakeholders. Below is a recommended structure.

- **Overview**
  - Summary of evidence leading to the test
  - Hypothesis
  - Result
- **Details**
  - Screenshots of the control and variations
  - Outline of the changes introduced
  - Type of test
  - Number of variations
  - Pages or area of the site targeted
  - Audience or segments targeted
  - Number of visitors per variation
  - Test duration and dates

- Results
  - Percentage or RPV difference
  - Statistical significance
  - Screenshot of the results
  - Annualized revenue impact on the business
  - Key learnings
  - Next steps

There are many benefits of distributing the results to your colleagues, including:

- They can learn about the value of split testing and see evidence triumphing over opinion.

- What you learn from the split test results, which is effectively how your online customers behave, can be shared and often used in other forms of marketing, such as stores, catalogues or direct marketing campaigns.

- It shows you are open and willing to share what you have learnt about the behaviour of your website visitors – whether or not the split test is positive.

- It's great to celebrate wins when your optimization efforts pay off and add real cash to the bottom line.

Finally, make sure to implement wins on the site. You'd be surprised how many times this fails to happen. That seems crazy – you're almost certainly going to make money from putting it live, and you even have an idea of just how much money you might make. So why does it not happen? Often it's because it's low on the list of priorities for the web developers. Sometimes it's because of internal politics and other times it just gets overlooked. The only thing worse than not testing at all, is to sit on winning tests without committing the changes live on the site in order to start realizing the gains.

Summary

Split testing is pivotal to e-commerce optimization. It's more than a mechanism that enables you to test hypotheses: it's one of the best inputs for data-backed decision-making.

There are several different types of tests, but A/B/*n* tests are the most common. Make sure you pick the appropriate type for your purpose.

In choosing a metric, it's important to get as close to revenue as possible. When the site does not have a lot of traffic, it may be difficult to use revenue goals. In this situation it may be better to opt for micro goals instead.

Split testing is grounded in statistical principles. Basic understanding of a few concepts will help you interpret test results correctly. Avoid being over-reliant on statistical significance and use other equally important data points to get a comprehensive and robust picture.

A test is not finished until results and discoveries have been documented. Even negative tests present valuable opportunities to learn, moving a step closer to a win. A winning test is one where you've learnt something valuable about your customers. Have a process in place to make sure that winning tests get put live on the site so that you can bank the gains.

Notes

1 Farris, P, Bendle, N, Pfeifer, P, Reibstein, D (2010) *Marketing Metrics: The definitive guide to measuring performance*, Pearson, New Jersey.

2 Experiment Engine, eCommerce A/B Test Data & Improved Process: When you win, you win big (Part 2), Available from: https://www.experimentengine.com/blog/2015/10/13/ecommerce-test-data-process-part2/ (accessed: 1 July 2016).

3 Experiment Engine, eCommerce A/B Test Data & Improved Process: when you win, you win big (Part 2), Available from: https://www.experimentengine.com/blog/2015/10/13/ecommerce-test-data-process-part2/ (accessed: 1 July 2016).

4 Conversation at Which Test Won, Berlin, October 2015.

5 Lee, D (2015) AB Testing: Test big to find your strategic optimal, available at: https://www.linkedin.com/pulse/ab-testing-test-big-find-your-strategic-optimal-daniel-analytics- (accessed: 1 July 2016).

6 Goodson, M (2014) Most Winning A/B Test Results are Illusory, Qubit, available from: http://www.qubit.com/sites/default/files/pdf/mostwinning-abtestresultsareillusory_0.pdf (accessed 12 July 16).

7 Optimizely (2016) A/B Test Sample Size Calculator, available from: https://www.optimizely.com/resources/sample-size-calculator/ (accessed: 1 July 2016).

8 Grace-Martin, K, The Effect Size: The most difficult step in calculating sample size estimates, available from: http://www.theanalysisfactor.com/sample-size-most-difficult-step (accessed: 1 July 2016).

9 Optimizely (2016) A/B Test Sample Size Calculator, available from: https://www.optimizely.com/resources/sample-size-calculator/ (accessed: 1 July 2016).

Personalization   10

What is personalization?

Personalization is an exciting approach to optimization that is becoming increasingly popular.[1] It involves serving a variation of web page (or web pages) to a defined subset of your visitors. That subset could be as small as one person. To allow you to assess the performance of a personalization experiment, a proportion of visitors see a non-personalized version, the 'holdback' segment.

The ultimate personalized web experience gives each visitor a unique journey based on who they are and how they have behaved previously. It is the online equivalent of walking into your favourite hotel, being recognized by the concierge and having the barman ask if you would like your 'usual'.

These kind of bespoke web experiences have been made possible by sophisticated technology platforms that use an array of complex algorithms. However, it is a misconception that all personalization is completely tailored to each individual visitor. The truth is that there is enormous potential to increase sales from simply segmenting your visitor types and offering something more relevant to each.

In fact, currently most web personalization falls into this category and there are lots of examples to show that it can give you a healthy uplift – although it is not a silver bullet and can't do magic.

Personalization is simply one approach you can adopt as part of a wider optimization strategy. So how do you integrate personalization and identify the most promising opportunities?

Different forms of personalization

To give your visitors a tailored experience you need to know *who* they are and *what* they do on your site.

There are two ways to capture information about who they are and what they do:

Anonymous data: your web analytics tool records 'anonymous variables'. These are either cookie-based or session-based.

An example of an anonymous variable about *who* they are might be whether the visitor is new or coming back for a return visit. An example of *what* they do would be whether they visited a particular product or category.

Since the data is anonymous you don't know the visitor's name, so they belong to a **segment** of your visitors.

Known data: data you have captured about your individual visitors and stored in an external data source is called 'known variables'. This can be information they have given you or that you know about them from other sources.

Known data about *who* they are might be their name and demographics, while known data about *what* they do includes previous purchase history.

This type of data is not anonymous; you can tie it back to the **individual** visitor.

We can use these four designations to create a universe of personalization opportunities for various segments and individuals:

- Who they are (known)
- Who they are (anonymous)
- How they behaved (known)
- How they behaved (anonymous)

Table 10.1   Examples – universe of data for personalization experiments.

	Anonymous variables	Known variables
Who your visitor is	Returning visitor Mobile device user On their 10th visit Has converted Referred by Facebook Browsing from Canada	Name Age Income Address Interested in windsurfing
What they did	Viewed 'sofas' category Signed up for e-mail newsletter Logged in to view previous orders Abandoned their basket	Bought four times in last 12 months, spending a total of £512 Shops both instore and online Typically orders two items and returns one

One of the most well-known forms of personalization is the Product Recommendation Engine (PRE). These software tools use algorithms to generate suggestions when a visitor is looking for a particular product. Created using anonymous variables, they show up on the site as images and messages like 'People who bought this also bought...'

PREs can also be used to give the customer recommendations based on known variables such as what they have bought in the past, even to the extent of creating for them a personalized homepage based on previous buying behaviour.

You can develop a PRE yourself or use one of the many commercially available engines from companies like Rich Relevance, Attraqt, Peerius and Barillance. In 2012 Amazon reported a 29 per cent increase in sales after introducing their own recommendation system.[2]

To offer personalized experiences using known variables such as a visitor's personal details requires investment in a personalization platform that can drill down to the level of the individual.

The mechanism that makes it possible to offer these types of experiences is a data layer. This is designed to integrate a number of data sources, such as a customer database, into the personalization platform.

These experiments tend to be harder and more expensive to implement.[3] Not only do they require sophisticated technology, but they also need considerable thought about the data layer's components and how the algorithm will work to ensure that the correct experiment is served to the right individual. Companies like Qubit, Optimizely, Monetate and Maxymiser offer personalization platforms that make setting up these personalization experiments more straightforward.

However, there are many other ways to do personalization without the use of complex algorithms. It's not essential to have reams of known data to create a basic personalized web experience. You can get decent results from making simple changes using just anonymous variables, such as location.

Location targeting

A very simple personalization technique is based on nothing more than the location from which the user is viewing the website. Some sites have reported an uplift in sales by showing images of local landmarks on their home page, such as the Eiffel Tower for users in Paris and the Statue of Liberty for users in New York.

Below is an example which takes it one step further and incorporates the weather where they happen to be. Leading men's clothing retailer, Burton

Figure 10.1   Personalizing the Burton homepage to show weather data to users in cold locations achieved a 11.6 per cent increase in conversion rate

SOURCE Image courtesy of Qubit

Figure 10.2   Boyle achieved a 5 per cent increase in new account creation by offering a personalized offer tailored specifically to new visitors

SOURCE Image courtesy of Qubit

personalized their home page by showing a different image whenever the temperature dropped below a certain level in the town where the user was browsing. A selection of warm clothing would appear alongside the symbol for snow as well as the name of the town and the local temperature.

New visitor

Anonymous Variables, like new or returning visitors, were also behind an effective project for Boyle Sports. Anyone visiting the site for the first time was given a personalized offer to encourage them to create an account.

When should you personalize?

Success stories like these mean that many companies are keen to offer visitors a personalized experience and there are now a host of technologies available to do this quickly and cheaply.

However, it is a mistake to jump straight on to the personalization bandwagon just because it looks like a way to make a fast buck. It only works when there are certain factors in place. Specifically there are three indicators that tell you when to put personalization high up on your shortlist of opportunities:

1 **Indicator 1: research uncovers a segmentation opportunity:** you discover that there is one segment of your visitors who seem to behave in a significantly different way. There is no basis for this apart from your observations but the insight is strong enough to warrant a test.

2 **Indicator 2: split testing reveals a segmentation opportunity:** when you analyse the results of a split test, you find markedly different results among different visitor segments.

3 **Indicator 3: your frequency of split testing wins starts to plateau or you notice your average uplift going down:** optimization is geared towards increasing sales for all visitors, so in a sense you are always optimizing for the 'average visitor'. This one-size-fits-all approach often does the job very well but there may come a time when you need to try a fresh approach.

If any of these apply to you, you should consider using personalization:

Indicator 1: Research-led segmentation opportunities

Imagine you discover that a high proportion of first-time visitors are unfamiliar with your brand and have some concerns about your products.

Table 10.2   Example of results from a Product Detail Page (PDP) split test showing differences in behaviour for new and returning visitors

	TOTAL	SEGMENT	SEGMENT
	All visitors	**New visitors**	**Returning visitors**
Unique visitors	995,000	497,500	497,500
Total revenue	£6,209,950	£1,813,950	£4,396,000
RPV - Control	£6.21	£3.31	£9.12
RPV - Experiment	£6.27	£3.99	£8.55
Uplift in RPV	1%	21%	–6%

Many of these first-time visitors land on your homepage. From this insight you might hypothesize that you need to give new visitors a personalized experience to educate them and reassure them.

Your chosen creative solution is to show a video of your CEO talking about why she started the business, the customer problems she wanted to solve and interviews with the committed customer service team. The video has been specifically made to allay fears and increase trust in your brand. This is an example of where you have discovered a personalization opportunity through research.

Indicator 2: Split test-led segmentation opportunities

Post-test segmentation lets you examine how different segments reacted differently to changes introduced in a split test. Integrate GA with the split test to identify segments that might respond to a personalized approach.

You need a sizeable segment to work on. For enterprises a substantial segment could represent just 5 per cent of your revenue, if you are a start-up it could be as high as 75 per cent of your revenue.

To show you how this works, the scenario below shows a split test around all visitors, not just a segment. Let's say the hypothesis was related to improvements to the Product Detail Page (PDP) and the experiment tested a revised layout. Separately, you have calculated the size of your segments for both new and returning visitors and are aware that both are substantial.

The data shows that while uplift in Revenue Per Visitor as a whole was only 1 per cent, there is a marked difference in the two segments of new visitors and returning visitors. The revenue uplift from new visitors who saw the experiment was much higher than from returning visitors. Armed with this knowledge, it may well be worth creating a personalized experience just for new visitors.

Indicator 3: Revitalizing a plateauing split testing programme

Plateauing can occur once you have addressed most of the opportunities on your list. When you reach the point where it's no longer enough to optimize for the average visitor, then personalization could get you good uplifts once again. As always, it's preferable that your experiments are grounded in objective research and analysis.

Designing a personalized experience

But what to test? The creative possibilities are endless and the technology to make it happen gets cheaper and easier all the time. There are a huge number of solutions so your biggest problem could be not the mechanics of personalization but deciding what unique experience to offer.

Before you invest a lot of time and effort into a personalization programme, bring some clarity to your decision making by asking yourself these three questions.[4]

- Who will see the experiment?
- What are they going to see?
- Where in the journey will they see it?

In the scenario above, where you have created a video specially for new visitors, the answer to the three W questions would be:

Q. Who is going to see this experiment?

A. New visitors

Q. What are they going to see?

A. A video about your business and your commitment to customer service

Q. Where in the visitor journey is this going to be shown?

A. At the beginning, on the homepage

If you can give clear, satisfactory answers to all three W questions there is a good chance that a personalized experience will have a positive impact and improve your website.

Technical options for personalization

In terms of the technology to power personalized experiments, you have two main options:

1 **Use your existing split test platform.** Just a little targeting is required to conduct basic personalization experiments. If, for example, you want to do something special for first-time visitors, then use the relevant segment in the platform. You may also be able to create custom segments by planting cookies and configuring the testing tool to recognize these.

2 **Use a specialist personalization platform.** If you want to run personalized experiments without needing to tie up your developer, or if you want to run more sophisticated tests, it's time to invest in a dedicated personalization platform. Vendors in this space include Optimizely, Qubit, Maxymiser and Adobe. They allow you to run several complex

experiments at the same time. Some of these platforms can also autosuggest segments for which it may be profitable to run experiments.

Although it is possible to run exciting, highly personalized web experiences, they are expensive, so you have to use them wisely to ensure a return on investment. It may be a good idea to involve a specialist agency in the initial stages. You may want to start off by going for the simple approach and even set custom segments to run a few basic personalization experiments. This gives you the chance to learn more about what personalization could offer your website visitors and decide at what point you want to make the investment in a sophisticated personalization platform.

How does personalization differ from split testing?

There are a number of similarities between personalization and split testing. Both require a hypothesis to be tested and shown to be valid or refuted. Both typically involve two versions and, in both, each version is shown to a particular set of users. When the test period has ended, both are reported using a standard metric such as RPV.

Where personalization experiments are different is when they use a data layer to deliver a bespoke experience born from the Known Data held on that individual. These types of experiments never really end – they run continually because you don't want your customer to be greeted by name one day and treated like a stranger the next.

Conventional split tests, on the other hand, typically end when they reach pre-agreed goals. At that point they will usually be stopped and hard-coded into the e-commerce platform.

Simultaneous testing and personalization

As you gain more experience in setting up split tests to test a hypothesis and then running personalized experiments on those visitor segments that performed well, you may wonder if it is possible to adopt these two approaches simultaneously.

If that thought has occurred to you, then you're in good company, as it can be highly profitable. The majority of organizations (84 per cent) see an increase in conversion rates when they combine A/B testing with web personalization, according to research.[5]

However, there are pitfalls if you're running a conventional split test and a personalization test at the same time, as you need to make sure that one doesn't skew the results of the other. To avoid this, you could allocate traffic to split testing and personalization as follows:

50 per cent of traffic available for split testing

50 per cent of traffic for your personalization experiments

For personalization experiments the traffic split between the experiment and the holdback segment will depend on whether the hypothesis that has prompted this experiment has already been tested in a split test or is a new hypothesis.

If you already have a positive result from a previous split test you might have an 80:20 split between experiment and holdback. This is because you have a higher level of confidence that this personalization experiment will generate an uplift. However, if this is a new, as yet untested hypothesis, based on research about a certain subset of your visitors, consider having a 50:50 split. You will get results more quickly because the holdback segment contains a bigger sample than in the 80:20 example.

As you become more confident in split testing, combining this with personalization allows you to have the advantages of optimizing for all visitors as well as offering a tailored experience for valuable visitor segments. Ensuring that the results from each type of testing don't skew each other is vital.

Summary

Whilst personalization is not a silver bullet, it can and should be an important part of your website optimization strategy. It offers you the opportunity to make the web experience more relevant to segments of your visitors, even down to individual users. The more relevant you make the experience, the better your website will convert visitors into customers. Personalization relies on what you know about who your website visitor is and how they behave on your site. Using anonymous and known variables can help you build both simple and complex personalization experiences.

Many companies have seen healthy uplift from running simple personalization experiments based on anonymous variables, like new and returning visitors, user location and visits to particular product categories.

Personalization opportunities can be discovered through research as well as by performing post-test segmentation analysis on previous tests. If you see the results from optimizing your website for all visitors starting to wane, consider using personalization to re-vitalize your website optimization efforts.

To design and launch a personalized experiment, you need to answer three questions – who will see, what will they see and where in the customer journey will they see the experiment.

You can adapt your split testing platform to serve simple personalization experiments, based on your anonymous data – who your visitors are and how they behave. Once you want to integrate customers, or external data, into your experiments, look at investing in a personalization platform. Many businesses have reported benefits from doing split testing and personalization simultaneously, and with careful separation of traffic you can do this easily without skewing your results from each.

Notes

1 Econsultancy (2016) Website Personalisation Buyers Guide, available from: https://econsultancy.com/reports/website-personalisation-buyers-guide/ (accessed: 1 July 2016).

2 Mangalindan, J (2012) Amazon's Recommendation Secret, available from: http://fortune.com/2012/07/30/amazons-recommendation-secret (accessed: 1 July 2016).

3 Econsultancy (2016) Website Personalisation Buyers Guide, available from: https://econsultancy.com/reports/website-personalisation-buyers-guide/ (accessed: 1 July 2016).

4 Marketo (2016) The 3 W's of Personalization, available from: https://www.marketo.com/slides-and-templates/the-3-ws-of-personalization/ (accessed: 1 July 2016).

5 Econsultancy (2015) Conversion Rate Optimisation Report 2015, available from: https://econsultancy.com/reports/conversion-rate-Optimisation-report/ (accessed: 1 July 2016).

Optimizing the optimization   11

Kaizen, the Japanese for 'improvement', is an approach to continuous improvement where small changes are constantly introduced in order to improve quality and efficiency. You can take the Kaizen mindset to optimize your own optimization process.

The measurement we use to assess overall performance of the optimization process is Compounded Annual Uplift. This takes into account the effectiveness of all your split-test results over the course of a year. You can leverage big gains in your annual results just by making small changes to three key levers. We call these 'Power Metrics', and they hold the key to exponentially improving the effectiveness of your entire optimization programme.

The three Power Metrics are:

1 **Test velocity** – How many split-tests you are launching (usually measured as tests per year).

2 **Win rate** – The number of tests per year that split-tests generate a positive uplift (usually expressed as a percentage)

3 **Average uplift** – The average size of uplifts of positive split-tests, in terms of RPV

Here's how it works in practice. Let's say this is your baseline performance:

Test velocity over the last 12 months	24 tests
Win rate	29% (7 tests were positive, 17 negative)
Average uplift per test	5.9%

Compounding the effects of the 7 positive tests, averaging a 5.9 per cent RPV uplift, generates a total compounded site-wide uplift over the last 12 months of 49%.

However, don't fall into the trap of thinking that this means a 49 per cent increase in sales. Extrapolating split-test results into predictable sales increases is notoriously difficult as we explained detail in Chapter 9.

Put simply, split-testing measures short-term changes in customer behaviour. Your test may run for a few weeks and you see increase in RPV increase. What it shows is how sales vary in that time period. After you have coded the experiment to be a permanent part of your site, the RPV uplift may not be the same as that observed during the test. There are other factors at play, including long-term changes in customer behaviour, as well as customer satisfaction and loyalty.

The value of the Compounded Annual Uplift lies in being a robust benchmark of your optimization programme.

To increase it, focus on those three power metrics – in other words, to run more split-tests – get more of those tests to be wins, and get your average win to be greater. You'll see an overall increase in your total figure.

So what would be the impact of an increase of just 10 per cent in each? It's shown in the table below.

You can see that those tiny changes in each area have had a profound effect on the Compounded Annual Uplift, which has gone up from 49 per cent to 64 per cent. This is a healthy indicator that your conversion programme is benefiting from optimizing your optimization.

This improvement is certainly worth having, but how do you improve each one of the three metrics? Here's how.

Power Metric 1 – How to increase your test velocity

There are a number of ways you can simply and easily increase the number of tests you are launching. By this we don't mean simply increasing the number of tests for the sake of it. Indulging in Random Acts of Testing (RATS), while increasing velocity will depress your win-rate

Table 11.1   An increase of just 10 per cent in each of your three power metrics leads to a 32 per cent improvement in total uplift

	Benchmark	10% improvement
Test Velocity in 12 months	24	26
Win Rate	29%	32%
Average Uplift	5.86%	6.44%
Compounded uplift over 12 months	49%	64%

and average uplift and ultimately reduce the profit of your optimization programme.

Here are five strategies you can use, without sacrificing the quality of your testing programme:

1 Keep filling your bucket of new ideas from the pipeline in your Optimization plan, so there's never a time when you are searching around for a hypothesis to test.

2 Work out how many 'slots' you have on your website to test. A slot is an area of your website. Most e-commerce websites have 7–10 slots on which you can test such as:

- Home/landing page
- Category page
- Product listing page (PLP)
- Product detail page (PDP)
- Search results page
- Basket page
- 1–4 checkout pages

When you add in your mobile website, you double the number of slots to 14–20.

Since it's best to avoid running more than one test on each area or slot at any one time, think of your tests like spaces in a car park. If you have a test running on one area, that is one of your car park spaces occupied. You won't be able to run another test on this area until the first test has been declared.

So it's vital to increase your test velocity so that you ensure you are testing on as many areas of the website as possible and are sure you have a new test ready to go as soon as each split-test is declared.

3 Developing complex tests takes time and money, so prioritize your hypotheses and launch simple-to-code tests first.

4 Run your split-tests only for the required amount of time. If you leave them running longer than necessary you are occupying one of your car parking spaces, and reducing the efficiency of your optimization programme.

5 Use a higher Minimum Detectable Effect (MDE). For example, instead of using a MDE of 3 per cent, increase it to 5 per cent or higher. This means your split testing tool won't detect results that are less than 5% and means you can make the best use of your available traffic and testing slots. For a more detailed explanation of MDE refer to Chapter 9.

Power Metric 2 – How to increase your win rate

If 100% of your split-tests are 'wins' we suspect that you either had a very poor website to begin with, or more likely, you are misinterpreting your split test results and declaring false positives. False positives look like 'wins', but on closer inspection of the data there is unlikely to be any real change to visitor behaviour. In fact, sometimes it could even have a have a damaging impact on sales.

Likewise, if only a small percentage of your split-tests are beating the control, then you also have a problem. The most important thing is to get your overall win rate i increasing from this low baseline.

There are three main approaches you can take to increasing the proportion of your split-tests that result in a positive uplift.

- Make sure your hypothesis development is informed by data and research, so that you avoid the RATs (Random Acts of Testing).

- Prioritize your hypotheses diligently – if you test an unimportant hypothesis then however good your creative execution is your win rate will be less than you could have achieved.

- Reduce the quantity of bolder tests – instead focus on incremental tests on areas of the website where you have generated solid results

Power Metric 3 – How to increase your average uplift

Increasing your uplift can be achieved in these ways:

- Continue to do further research – both qualitative and quantitative – to uncover users' motivations and goals. Your website visitors and customers change constantly, along with your competitors, and there is always more you can learn and test.

- Review the results from previous split tests. This will help you identify where you might be able to get a better result by changing a few elements.

- Refine your approach to prioritization. Examine which tests produced healthy uplifts and how you originally prioritized them. Also look at tests that didn't produce a positive result and what you can learn about how your prioritized these tests.

You can then compare these costs against the increases in online sales you believe you program has generated. Of course the gains you believe you have made from optimization always need to be higher than your costs. In addition, you have the less measurable, yet invaluable, benefit of the insights you have uncovered about your website visitors and customers – knowledge that will serve you well across the whole company.

Summary

Recognize that the process of optimization can be optimized itself. Your benchmark metric for this is the 12-month total Compounded Uplift.

You can improve your optimization efforts exponentially by focusing on three key metrics:

- Test Velocity – the number of tests you run each year
- Win Rate – the number of tests that show a positive uplift
- Average Uplift

There are a number of strategies that you can use to successfully increase these metrics. Most of them are rooted in diligent research, analysis and prioritization, as well as careful planning of logistics.

An increase in any one of these areas will improve your Annual Compounded Uplift. An increase in all three will optimize your optimization exponentially. This is not a measure of how much your revenue will increase, but a robust way to benchmark the fundamental effectiveness of your CRO programme.

People and culture 12

This book is intended as a guide for anyone wanting to do Conversion Rate Optimization (CRO) themselves.

However, it can also be used if you want to know more about the nuts and bolts of CRO, so that you can understand better what your optimization team do and how to get the best out of them.

How to find, select and motivate in-house conversion optimizers

An in-house conversion optimizer may need to fulfil a number of roles:

- Researcher – using a variety of data sources to build a rich picture of visitors and customers
- Data analyst – analysing data from the website and interpreting the results of split tests
- Project manager – managing a team of specialists; using a structured data-driven process as well as engaging with stakeholders and presenting results

Skills and traits of talented conversion optimizers

A key skill these people have is the ability to switch comfortably between left- and right-brain thinking.

Left-brain thinking

Left-brain thinking is concerned with logic, rationality and working with numbers. Analytical skills are a huge part of what an optimizer needs to have in their toolkit. For a recent client, one of our optimizers:

Figure 12.1   Left- and right-brain thinking

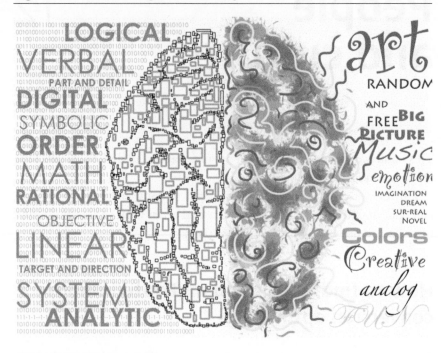

SOURCE Rakkandee/Shutterstock

- Analysed 20 million Google Analytics and IBM Digital Analytics sessions
- Observed website visitors for 20+ hours during usability testing
- Examined the click pattern from 175,000 sessions using heatmaps, scroll maps, confetti maps and others
- Read and analysed 20,000 survey responses
- Performed 443 navigation tasks using specialized tools
- Read numerous live chat transcripts
- Conducted five store visits, interviewing store managers and shop floor staff
- Interviewed the Customer Service team and the live chat operators

To cope with this amount of data, an optimizer needs advanced information-processing and number-crunching skills. The process of prioritizing large numbers of possible website improvements to create an Optimization Plan requires focus and independent thought. To accurately interpret a completed split test your optimizer needs both analytics skills and a thorough grounding in statistics.

Right-brain thinking

Contrast this attention to detail with the thought processes dominant in right-brain thinking.

First is the ability to build relationships with the broader internal team (developers, copywriters, managers, co-workers and business leaders, etc). They also need to be able to quickly establish rapport and show empathy with people when using research methods like moderated usability testing. This should be allied with creative skills: coming up with imaginative but relevant solutions to the identified opportunities. It's one thing to identify a conversion killer, it takes a leap of imagination to understand how to translate this problem into a new, improved version.

- What will the wireframe look like?
- What copy is required?
- How will someone navigate this new page?

These are examples of creative questions the optimizer will deal with. Understanding the fundamentals of consumer psychology, covered in Chapter 3, plays an important part here.

Presenting the results of research and split tests also requires creativity: to put oneself in the position of your audience and tailor the presentation to their needs. Here the focus is on condensing vast amounts of research into a few powerful ideas that have been tested scientifically and then presenting the results in non-technical language that illuminates the insight gained.

To bring left- and right-brain thinking together, an effective optimizer has to be detail-obsessed, familiar with the minutiae of the visitor experience, while at the same time holding onto the bigger picture. They understand that buying online is a complex process involving your offer and how it's positioned in the market, user experience, persuasion techniques and a number of psychological factors.

Other traits include a passion for CRO, zealot-like determination to be continually improving and a drive to translate optimization into hard cash for the business. Overwhelmingly, talented optimizers are both curious and humble: they know what they don't know and are always looking to learn more.

Being an attractive employer

The competition for optimizers is intense, so think about this question your ideal candidate will be asking him or herself: 'Given the competition for my talents, why would I join your company?' If this sounds similar to the principles of creating a strong value proposition that we discussed in Chapter 5, then you're right. The technique works just as well for recruiting your team as it does for recruiting customers.

Find out what optimizers are looking for in an employer. Reach out to communities in relevant LinkedIn groups and the blogosphere. Study how other companies looking for the same sort of person are defining their value proposition. Is yours clear and compelling?

Ask your existing team why they enjoy working for your business and use that in your job ad. Being specific when communicating your value proposition adds credibility. For example, instead of 'We are committed to your professional development' consider: 'Last year each member of our team received on average 112 hours of training, that's nearly four weeks of solid investment in you – we are committed to your development.'

Remote working

Chances are that your ideal optimizer is not living nearby. They may be located in a different country, a different time zone even. If you want to employ the best, consider the adaptations you may need to make – technology, team and processes – to allow a remote worker to be an effective team player. Far better to get the most talented optimizer to work for you and make the necessary adjustments than to choose someone on the basis of their proximity.

Finding the right person

Simply advertising the role might not attract enough experienced individuals. Another option is to approach people directly. Conversion optimization covers many disciplines and talented optimizers are always soaking up new knowledge and sharing what they have learnt, so look out for people who are active in public forums, commenting and sharing their knowledge.

Many conversion agencies publish blogs with an active comments section – eg ConversionXL, WiderFunnel, Unbounce Conversion Scientist, Occams Razor, Get Elastic, Which Test Won, Marketing Experiments, Future Now, and Online Behaviour. Testing platform providers – Qubit, Maxymiser, Monetate, Optimizely, Convert, Visual Website Optimizer and Adobe – provide similar forums.

There are LinkedIn groups for CRO and a Slack channel on CRO.

Before approaching candidates, create a survey for interested individuals to complete as part of the selection process. Questions could include:

- Please provide 2–3 examples of how you have created impressive results for online businesses.
- Tell us about your experience of:
  - Direct response marketing and copywriting.
  - Designing / wireframing high-converting web pages.
- Ask about level of experience (extensive, some or none) with the tools used in your organization: analytics packages, testing platforms, voice-of-customer tools, statistics, JavaScript and facilitation of usability sessions.

To form a richer picture about a candidate, we set up a voicemail account and ask candidates to phone in after they have completed the survey. For us, this part of the process is as important as their responses to the survey. On the voicemail the prospective candidates are asked a number of questions:

1 Why are you applying for this role?

2 What has been your greatest achievement to date?

3 Tell us about a time when you overcame a difficulty; what was it and how did you overcome it?

Listening to a candidate's tone of voice and how they handle these questions, with little time to prepare, will tell you a lot about them.

Having defined your value proposition and set up your survey and voicemail account, you can now start approaching possible candidates. Create a shortlist of those who responded to your contact, completed your survey and left you a voicemail. The next stage is to hold individual interviews and talk through the answers they gave in their survey response.

Focus particularly on the metrics applicants are using to explain the results they have created – is this site-wide revenue uplift, or is it just progression to next step in the customer journey, reducing bounce rate on a landing page or increasing e-mail sign-up rates? We have had some experience of applicants exaggerating the significance of the results they have created.

If relevant, explore how a remote working environment could fit in with your business. What experience do they have of building relationships remotely? What challenges do they face working remotely? Could they come and spend a week in the office, at least initially?

Try to discover what effort they make to stay up to date, what was the last new tool or research technique they used? Do they have a clear sense of what they don't know and what plans have they got to address this?

If you feel confident about their track record, how they would work with you and their commitment to keeping at the top of their game, the next stage is a practical test. We ask candidates to review a particular web page. Along with it we provide some basic data. We ask them to come up with a wireframe, explain their thinking and the data on which they have based these recommendations.

You can develop your own criteria for evaluating applications but we pay particular attention to:

- a demonstration of analytical thinking
- the logic of their arguments
- an ability to communicate clearly

Then hold a group interview with individuals who make the practical test stage. We have done this successfully on Google Hangouts, with four interviewers and a similar number of candidates. It can be telling to see how candidates react to a competitive selection process.

How to keep your in-house optimizer motivated

For a single in-house optimizer the job could be lonely and isolating, with no one to bat around ideas and hypotheses. At the same time, talented optimizers value autonomy. Motivation and retention requires that you manage their need for community and independence simultaneously. They also have an insatiable thirst for knowledge and for knowing that what they are doing is making a difference to the bottom line. To keep them motivated, ensure there are processes in place that allow them to:

- Spend time acquiring knowledge and being part of the conversion community
- Go on training courses, subscribe to paid-for courses and attend events
- Present your company's results at conferences and spark debate and interaction with their peers
- Work flexibly – from home, from remote locations and from the office when the need is there
- Allocate a proportion of their time to work on their own project, as companies like 3M and Google do

Having spoken to many optimizers, as well as those who recruit for these roles, one of the most common criticisms of employers is that firms do not fully understand what optimization is and what it can do for the business. Consequently, optimizers are directed to work on parts of the site where there is little evidence of it being a real opportunity. Or there is a lack of support for testing controversial areas where an opportunity has been identified. Before hiring an optimizer, you and management should agree on the scope of the role.

Obstacles to a culture of optimization

Finding and motivating a talented optimizer is one factor in the success of your optimization programme; another one is to build and reinforce a culture of optimization. So what are some of the benefits of having a culture of optimization?

- You grow your business more quickly
- You spend less time in endless internal debates
- You learn continuously
- You get focused on what really matters

A number of obstacles can prevent your organization from becoming data-driven and having an optimization mindset, which should be tackled first.[1] In this section we'll examine cognitive biases that can impact the individual, particularly your optimizer, as well as the obstacles your organization might face in terms of embedding an optimization culture.

Obstacles faced by individuals

When we are making judgements and decisions about the world around us, we like to think that we are objective and logical. Unfortunately, the reality is that our judgements and decisions are often impaired by errors and influenced by a wide variety of biases. These are called cognitive biases and can have a detrimental impact on an optimization process reliant on making judgements on huge quantities of data. By being aware of them you have a better chance of reducing their impact. Here are 11 biases we believe are most relevant to website optimization:

- **Belief bias** – we often accept invalid data to support a judgement based on our own beliefs. Believing something to be the case doesn't make it true. As much as possible be aware of the role of your own beliefs in reaching a decision.

- **Certainty bias** – in a perfectly rational world, we would value equally a change of probability of one going from 0 per cent to 10 per cent as we would from, say 45 per cent to 55 per cent. In fact we don't, we value certainty differently, depending on the starting point. This often results in us being more risk averse as we experience more disquiet as certainty diminishes, even if the less probable situation could benefit us more.

- **Confirmation bias** – sometimes one theory, or hypothesis, dominates our thoughts so strongly it becomes a preconception; so much so that we don't even realize there are alternatives – or even look for them. This means we could easily overlook data or conclusions that fly in the face of this preconception.

- **Congruence bias** – though similar to confirmation bias, congruence bias is concerned with the risk in optimization that we only split test one possible hypothesis, when in fact there are other possible hypotheses that may have been more valid and worthy of testing.

- **Dunning-Kruger bias** – this is where people who are 'incompetent' are more likely to be confident in their actions because they don't know what they don't know. So when recruiting for an optimizer ask them about areas where they feel less competent and be cautious of people who claim expertise in every area.

- **Framing bias** – we will often react to choice based on whether the outcome has been presented or 'framed' as a loss or a gain. Even small changes to how these outcomes are framed can have a profound impact on the choices we make and the risk we will tolerate.

- **Fundamental attribution error (FAE)** – this is where we give undue importance to people's characters and intention, rather than unconnected external factors. For example, if your checkout is causing users frustration, some might blame their 'stupidity' rather than accept how difficult the site is to use.

- **Hindsight bias** – sometimes called the 'knew it all along' effect, this is the tendency to see an event, after it has occurred, as predictable. This bias can often be seen in the analysis of medical experiments, judicial systems and historians writing about past events. For CRO this might mean positive tests are less carefully scrutinized than negative tests, because the result, in 'hindsight', was predictable and therefore less worthy of analysis and challenge.

- **Information bias** – sometimes we continue to collect more and more information on the basis that more is better and the additional data will lead to a more informed decision. When you are investing more time in collecting larger data sets be clear as to exactly what question you are trying to answer and whether this new data will help you achieve this.

- **Narrative fallacy** – a common tendency many of us have is to try and explain why something has occurred; we seek to provide a 'logical' link between two facts. Explanations bind facts together and yet this explanation may be incorrect. For example in the case of a split test, the only data that is known is the split test result, providing a narrative is just conjecture.

- **Self-serving bias** – this tendency arises out of a need to bolster our self-esteem by claiming 'success' to be down to our own qualities or traits; with 'failure' we are more likely to blame this on external factors. To work effectively in CRO, divorce yourself from your need for self-esteem and avoid being emotionally invested in the results of your split tests.

Whenever we are presented with information, we are prone to cognitive bias – and more than one at a time. Think about how you can counter these biases. Remember data is neutral but it is the way we process information that can have a significant impact on the validity of our decisions.

Obstacles faced by organizations

Three of the most powerful obstacles you may face in embedding a culture of optimization in your organization include:

1 The impact of a top-down organizational hierarchy

2 Internal competition

3 Lack of understanding about data and statistics and reliance on gut instinct

Let's look at how these obstacles are caused and their impact.

Top-down organizational hierarchies

As senior managers climb the organizational hierarchy, they tend to spend more time managing those with direct contact with the customer and less time with customers themselves. While power rests with the manager, insight about the customer's needs and motivations are further down the organization. Rigid organizational hierarchies, where there is little sharing of knowledge between those leading the business and those interacting with customers, represents an obstacle to optimization. Decisions about the way to treat customers can be disconnected from what customers need. We have seen e-commerce teams 'hide' controversial split tests from the rest of the organization in case senior managers, unfamiliar with the reasons behind the test, choose to stop the test prematurely.

Internal competition

Competition can arise between departments when objectives, measures and incentives do not align. This lack of alignment can turn friends into foes as well as undermine efforts to collaborate.[2] Often this lack of cooperation goes hand in hand with departments not sharing valuable information with others. As an agency we have seen many departmental battles over what should appear on the home page, each department determined to fight for their right for equal prominence. We have also seen store managers reluctant to direct in-store customers to the website as this online purchase wouldn't be reflected in store sales.

Lack of understanding about data and statistics

As more organizations aspire to be 'data driven' and the volume of available data increases exponentially, research indicates that managers' data literacy has not kept pace.[3] Even when they believe they are making decisions based on data, the interpretation is flawed. When reviewing new clients' previous split test results, we often find that wins have been declared prematurely. In some cases, a senior manager had intervened and stopped the test, based on his/her opinion that the test had produced a 'good result'.

Successful optimization cultures

Successful optimization cultures share seven things in common:[4]

1 **Data is shared, and shared widely** – rather than being 'owned' by departments. Without a commitment to data-sharing practices, data hoarding results, a richer picture fails to be grasped and opportunities are missed.

2 **Broad data literacy** – in order for a data-informed culture to flourish, senior managers need training to understand the nuances, terminology and inferences of statistical analysis. There are many free courses available on Coursera, Udacity, the Khan Academy and others.

3 **Goals-first culture** – optimization is for a purpose, an over-arching mission. A strategic vision allows the optimization process to work towards this goal. At AWA our mission is 'to make buying easier' – it focuses all our efforts. BMW's is The Ultimate Driving Machine, and it drives many of its engineering processes. Zappos' is 'To Provide the Best Customer Service Possible'.

4 **Inquisitive, questioning culture** – frank and open debate about the data, rather than the personalities or layers of hierarchies involved, allows a far more 'scientific' evaluation of the 'experiments' and the 'results'. This experimentation mindset can help to eliminate the egos often present in organizational improvement projects.

5 **Iterative, learning culture** – using the language of 'learning' rather than 'failure' or 'success' allows you to focus on what you can learn from each experiment and to continue the process of iterating and optimizing.

6 **Anti-HIPPO culture** – senior managers who continue to adopt a decision-making style that is based on their experience, preconceived notions and their gut, without regard to the available data will undermine successful data-informed cultures.

7 **Data leadership** – successful businesses 'compete on analytics' and leaders set an example in their use and promotion of data-informed decision-making. This means providing the tools, training, but, most importantly, recruiting other senior managers through celebrating wins – however small they may appear at first.

Case Study: So what does a culture of optimization actually look like?

This 350-year-old bank, which serves over 24 million customers across the globe, adopted a unique approach to how they embedded a culture of optimization. Each conversion manager is responsible for one of the 38 key customer journeys important to the bank. The bank labelled these conversion managers as 'Superstar DJs'. Weekly updates to the organization, as well as announcing wins and learnings, were peppered with dodgy puns and suggested soundtracks.

The conversion team went on roadshows to different bank locations to talk about their successes, wearing 'on tour' t-shirts, complete with venues and dates – just like the real thing. To promote competitions between the 'DJs' a 'chart' was published showing the best-performing split test. Stakeholders from outside the team were 'given' split tests as their own with access to the testing platform so they could easily monitor its performance. In this way senior managers, from outside the digital and analytics team, were able to grasp the importance of a testing culture to the bank – and get the chance to briefly join the troop of Superstar DJs.

'The way you are bringing this to life is nothing short of brilliant,' one senior manager commented.

Embedding an optimization culture is about recognizing the obstacles that affect both the individual, such as cognitive biases, as well as the organization – the negative impact of hierarchies, internal competition and the lack of understanding about data. The case study of the international bank shows how such an optimization culture can be both exciting and creative.

When to outsource

Sometimes it is not possible to recruit an in-house optimizer because of barriers such as headcount budget, inflexibility about remote working or the inability to find the right candidate. An external resource or agency can help in a number of different ways:

- You are growing rapidly, website traffic is growing quickly and you realize you have the financial resources but not the time to invest in conversion optimization. A third-party can start working alongside you to turn this burgeoning traffic into correspondingly higher conversion rates. Also high-growth companies are often focused on growth and may overlook some conversion issues that no one else has had time to address.

- Your digital team is young and, although enthusiastic, is inexperienced with conversion optimization. This might be the time to consider an agency that will help you get off to a flying start, and over time transfer knowledge to your team as they see how the agency does what it does. Make sure the agency you choose has experience of knowledge transfer and is able to provide mentoring or coaching services as your need for direct assistance starts to taper off.

- Alternatively you might have been optimizing your website for quite some time and starting to see your results plateau. This is the time to engage with an agency that can provide a fresh perspective and develop a completely new Optimization Plan so you have a new set of optimization opportunities on which your in-house team can focus.

- You may be expanding into new, international territories, where the culture is different and the needs of these website visitors and customers will not match those from your domestic market. Many companies have simply translated their current website into an international version, without fully understanding the differences between cultures and approaches to online buying. An agency with international optimization experience would be a good use of resources in leveraging the investment you are making in these new markets.

- Likewise, if you are creating a new customer journey, as in creating a new range of products or services, then it makes sense to bring in an agency to do the research on how a fresh set of visitors might respond to your new merchandise or services.

- Finally, if you are based in a rural location it is going to be challenging to find experienced conversion optimizers on your doorstep. You may also struggle to find talented copywriters, designers and developers who have experience of optimization projects. In this case bringing in an agency on a monthly-retainer basis is the best opportunity for getting an optimization programme in place.

Summary

Talented optimizers are skilled at using both left-brain (analytical and data-driven) and right-brain (creative and empathetic) thinking styles. They are marked out with traits such as humility, curiosity, persuasiveness, being process-oriented and detail-obsessed. As people they are determined, passionate and have a thorough grounding in consumer psychology and web technologies. The competition for their talent is unsurprisingly intense.

To compete for this talent, focus your attention on what makes you stand out as an employer. Use conversion forums to discover what it takes to be an employer for which optimizers want to work. Compare the proposition offered by other companies looking for this resource and be specific as to why you would be an ideal fit. Use a structured selection process to evaluate the claims made by your candidates, as well as offer the chance to show how they would optimize a real site.

Being data-driven and embedding a culture of optimization poses challenges both for individuals and the organization. Cognitive (such as congruence, self-serving and information) biases can sway an individual's understanding of what the data really means. Organizations are often faced with issues around top-down hierarchies, internal competition and a lack of data literacy at senior level. We propose a seven-point model of a successful optimization culture, and showed how an international bank re-positioned conversion optimizers as Rock Star DJs.

Finally, there may be times when it makes sense to outsource conversion optimization to a third party. This may be because the business is in a high-growth phase, you are based in a location where few conversion optimizers live, you have an inexperienced conversion team, your current results have started to plateau or you may be expanding into new territories or building new customer journeys.

Notes

1 Lewin, K (1964) *Field Theory in Social Science: Selected theoretical papers*, Harper and Row, Washington DC.

2 Pfeffer, J and Sutton, R (2000) *The Knowing-Doing Gap: How smart companies turn knowledge into action*, Harvard Business Press, Boston.

3 Croll, A and Yoskovitz (2012) *Lean Analytics*, O'Reilly, Sebastopol, California.

4 Anderson, C (2015) *Creating a Data-Driven Organization*, O'Reilly, Sebastopol, California.

Multilingual conversion optimization

Welcome visitors from afar

If 95 per cent of your visitors don't buy in your home country, even fewer will buy from the sites you're operating abroad. So, what can you do about it?

The good news is that an optimization process is just as effective for sites in other countries. People may speak a different language and have different cultural expectations but fundamentally they still buy the same way.

Many of the principles covered in earlier chapters can still be applied. The skill lies in knowing how to adapt the tools and techniques to differences in culture, taste, ways of doing business, expectations around customer service, communication preferences, visual language, lifestyles, working patterns and more.

Cross-cultural design experts Marcus and Gould summed it up well when they said, 'Consider your favourite *e-commerce* [added by author] website. How might this website be understood and used in New York, Paris, London, Beijing, New Delhi or Tokyo, assuming that adequate verbal translation were accomplished? Might something in its metaphors, mental model, navigation, interaction or appearance confuse, or even offend or alienate, a user?'[1]

There are a number of steps you can take to ensure your e-commerce website converts across different national audiences.

Cultural sensitivity as competitive advantage

National audiences have strong preferences for certain types of structure, design and navigation. For example, a study of the 100 most popular Chinese and American e-commerce websites found clear differences between the two countries:

- Chinese sites use a greater number of colours than their US counterparts
- Active banners and animations were used approximately 10 times more on Chinese sites than US websites
- Chinese sites feature a greater variety and intensity of layout elements, with an emphasis on 'squareness' to separate the various areas
- US sites favour image-based navigation, whilst Chinese sites tend to feature text-based navigation

Despite these embedded cultural norms, transnational internet giants, such as Amazon and Ebay, usually use the same navigation, home page, interface and corporate design in all the countries in which they operate.

If the international markets you serve include global competitors like these, then you could find optimization opportunities by being more sensitive to local culture.

However, if your resources are limited, take the time to examine whether there is a solid business case for expending effort on optimizing your international site(s). There may be more lucrative opportunities closer to home.

To get an idea of whether it's worth your time and effort to optimize some or all of your international sites, here are some questions to consider:

- What is the rate of e-commerce growth in my domestic and international markets?
- What is the difference in absolute numbers of online buyers in my markets?
- How do my traffic levels, device usage, conversion rate, AOV and RPV compare between my different e-commerce websites?
- To what extent are the results from my optimization efforts in my domestic market still growing or are they starting to plateau?
- How likely are consumers in my international market to buy online from a non-domestic brand? (For example, UK online buyers are nearly twice as likely to buy from a 'foreign' website as French or German consumers.[2])
- Which would make me more money – a 20 per cent RPV increase from one of my international sites or 5 per cent from my domestic one?
- Who are the dominant online players in my international markets and what is their rate of growth?

There are no right or wrong answers in this list. Simply asking the questions will help you gain clarity and focus.

Our approach to multilingual optimization

Having optimized a number of international websites we have seen first-hand the value of using a structured process and how it needs to be adapted for a foreign site. Most of the adaptations to the process are in the Research phase, because of the differences in language and culture.

Hiring a foreign speaker to help you with e-commerce optimization

If you don't have local staff you will to need to hire a foreign language speaking collaborator who has an understanding of the way the web works in that particular territory. Always insist that they are a native speaker of the country or region where the site is based as this person will play a number of roles, including:

- Translating between English and the foreign language and checking quality of translation performed by tools and third parties
- Setting up research tools to work on your international website
- Helping you to relate the analytics data to particular webpages
- Assisting you in the development of customer personas
- Analysing your competitors in the international market
- Analysing online and e-mail survey results completed by your international website visitors and customers
- Carrying out remote moderated usability with foreign usability testers
- Gathering feedback on the wireframes and artwork from other foreign language speakers

Your foreign collaborator should ideally have the following skills and background:

- Intelligent, articulate and curious – and willing to be led by evidence over opinion
- A keen user of the internet and familiarity with buying online
- Experience of web analytics, user experience (often called UX) and direct marketing
- Able to explain the differences between websites in your international territory and websites from your country

- Fluent in English – both written and verbal
- A familiarity with Excel and other data analysis tools
- Able to analyse large amounts of unstructured data (eg open-ended survey responses) and produce accurate analyses of key trends
- Able to build rapport with usability testers and tactfully and gently encourage testers to share the frustrations they are experiencing with your international website
- Able to be available at key points of the day for you to communicate – this is important given the time zone difference

We would recommend that your collaborator is resident in your international territory, so that they are fully immersed in the culture.

There are a number of places you can look to recruit this type of help, such as recruitment websites like UpWork and PeoplePerHour. Before offering your chosen candidate the role, ask him or /her to perform tests such as:

- Analysing the responses of an online or e-mail survey you have already performed on your domestic website and reporting their findings. Generally around 400 responses is sufficient.
- Explaining the differences between e-commerce websites in your international territory and your country.
- Summarizing insights from a number of panel-based usability videos of your website.

Translation

To speed up the data gathering process there may be times when it is appropriate to use translation services – either online services or agencies – but we recommend using your foreign collaborator to check the quality of any translated text.

For copy that is going to appear on the website, as part of a test, always have it translated from the source language into the translator's mother tongue. This gives you a more profound and nuanced translation, not only of the linguistics but also cultural understanding.

Even at the level of simple translation things can go wrong. Witness the offence (and hilarity) caused when, in 2011, American Airlines introduced its new first-class leather seats in Mexico with a literal translation of their tagline 'Fly in Leather', which in Spanish means 'fly naked'.[3]

But it's not just the language you need to consider when carrying out localization. Cultural, religious and political sensitivities also come into play. When Gap introduced a range of high-end jeans, called '1969' it did not think to alter this name for other cultures. While the year 1969 in the United States was one of political change and hope, for the Chinese this year came at the end of the Cultural Revolution, a part of the country's history that many Chinese customers were keen to forget.

Contrast this with the efforts made by Apple to get things right. When deciding whether or not to roll out its 'Macs are cooler than PCs' advertising campaign in Japan, Apple reflected on the differences between Japanese and North American customers. For the Japanese 'trashing' your competition is not considered acceptable. Rather than repeat the ad verbatim, Apple focused on the theme that PCs were more for office use, while Macs were more for personal and weekend use. The message was well received and Apple reaped the rewards.

Adaptations to the set-up and tool phase

Using research tools to gather both voice-of-customer data, as well as hard data (such as analytics, heatmaps, eye-tracking studies) is as vital for an international website as it is for one in your own language.

Many of the research and analysis tools we have mentioned earlier have versions suitable for international sites.

Figure 13.1   Chinese version of a pop-up survey

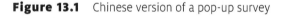

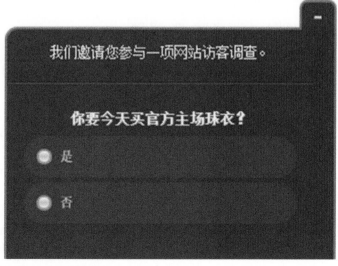

SOURCE Image courtesy of Qualaroo

Adaptations to the research phase

Customer journey mapping

As you may remember from Chapter 4, the start of the Research and Analysis phase is the mapping of the customer journey, using web analytics data.

With a website in a different language, with page titles possibly in an unfamiliar alphabet, you will need the help of your foreign collaborator to ensure you have correctly identified the right page in the conversion journey and clearly understand which is the next page in the process.

When we are working on an international website project we will often print out each page of the customer journey and mount it on the wall – it makes sense to capture the pages from key journeys such as device or traffic source and add in the dropout rate data.

One of the most important analyses is to compare the customer journey of visitors to your international site and domestic one. It may well be that international customers are falling out of the journey at different points and different rates. Even if your international visitors are falling out of the journey at the same point, it may be for very different reasons.

Persona development

Given the cultural differences with your domestic website visitors, creating accurate personas to help with the optimization process is vital. The method of creating them is the same as described in Chapter 4, but in summary, the important data to capture are:

- Personas – context, behaviours and attitude
- Goals – what are your international visitors' core motivations?
- Scenarios – stories that outline the sequence of activities carried out by the user to achieve their goal

Having created these personas, compare them with the personas of visitors to your domestic site. The analysis will highlight key differences that you can use to further your research activities.

As an example, one of our clients, a Spanish football club, sold team merchandise, such as apparel, souvenirs and the team strip on a number of their international websites. In our research we discovered two distinct personas. Spanish customers were already members of the football club, who often had bought the team strip and were looking for other branded

Figure 13.2   Chinese version of a tool to recruit customers for a live usability study

SOURCE Image courtesy of Ethnio

merchandise. Given the state of the Spanish economy at the time, many of them were looking to use their member's discount to grab a bargain. Chinese consumers, on the other hand, were looking to tap into this famous European football brand and wanted reassurance that the goods were genuine European merchandise and not counterfeit.

Research with international visitors

With multilingual optimization you use the same research techniques you would normally, but you may need to make some adjustments and use your native language speaker to help you with the research.

This is especially true of remote moderated usability testing (RMUT). You may need help in drafting the screener questions you want to ask potential usability testers, and these will need to be translated.

The table below lists some of the research techniques you might decide to use on your international website and what sort of help you are likely to need from your foreign collaborator.

The last two activities – reviewing split tests from the domestic site and facilitating remote moderated usability sessions – require more detailed explanation, as they are critical to the optimization process.

Table 13.1　Adaptations to Research phase for multilingual optimization

Research technique	Help required from foreign language speaker
Live chat transcript analysis	Reviewing the translation of live chat transcripts, creation of word cloud, identification of major themes and languages used, presentation of results of analysis and insight
Merchandising analytics	Help identify products and categories, work with you to perform look-to-book and price-point analysis
Customer service staff interviews	Getting answers to your questions, asking their own as well, checking quality of translated interviews
Analysis of emails to customer service team	Acting as a data analyst, reading a sample of customer service e-mails and presenting back to you an analysis of common themes and issues
Social media analysis	Track social media comments (either critical or glowing) and identify themes
Value proposition and competitor analysis	Advice on competitors' value propositions; critiquing their strengths and weaknesses
Heuristics	Using a heuristic framework to work with your collaborator to generate insights
Search marketing analysis	Reviewing with you the translation of the most common (including highest and lowest converting) paid and natural search terms being used, so you can analyse the bounce rate, conversion rate and revenue
Website analytics	To make best use of your collaborator's time analyse as much as you can without his/her support and then make a list of questions you want to work on together to analyse
Usage of on-site search	Reviewing with you the translation of most common, highest and lowest converting onsite search terms
Browser investigation	No input required to identify whether particular browsers suffer from lower levels of conversion
Customer immersion	Ask your collaborator to make a recording of themselves buying from the website and annotate the video with difficulties experienced and his/her reflections. Carry this through to videoing or photographing the package when it arrives, and returning it

Heat and scroll maps	Review these together to understand what words, graphical elements and navigation options are being clicked or scrolled to, and those that are not, and what cultural norms may be underlying that behaviour
Look-to-book ratios	Examining, together, those products, identified from your analysis, that have above average page views but below average add-to-basket ratio with a view to understanding cultural reasons why they are poor sellers
Copy review	Reviewing with you the translation of key pages, as well as the product copy of the highest and lowest converting products, so you see to what extent the copy is helping to overcome website visitors' objections identified from your research
Form analysis	Examining together the drop-off rates by form field
Site speed tests	No help required
Eye-tracking studies	Reviewing these together to understand what words, graphical elements and navigation options are receiving considerable attention and those that are not, and the cultural reasons for this
Sales staff interviews	Conducting and recording interviews and arranging for the translation of these interviews
Analysis of customer reviews	Arranging for the translation, as well as analysis, of key trends, phrases and themes
Panel-based or automated usability testing	In this case your collaborator is acting as translator of videos sourced from a panel of usability testers, translating the commentary so that videos can be watched by a non-Chinese speaker
Review of previous split tests performed on the domestic site	Reviewing the new web page created and the results from the split test on the domestic site, analysing the strength of the hypothesis being tested – see section below
Remote moderated usability testing	Recruiting moderated usability testers, running these sessions and translating the commentary so that videos can be watched by a non-Chinese speaker – see section below

Reviewing the domestic site split tests

Why this is important is because you can short-cut a lot of your split testing on the foreign site if you find out that it is tightly coupled to your home site. That means that something that works well at home will also work well abroad.

If you are fortunate enough to discover this phenomenon in your business, your job becomes a lot easier because it means that if you get a win on the domestic site, you can quickly and easily replicate that success abroad.

Tightly coupled optimization is more likely to occur when the national cultures of the domestic and international website visitors are similar, such as the UK and the Netherlands.

To be certain that you are lucky enough to have a process that is tightly coupled you need to run the same seven to ten of the winning tests from your domestic site on your international site: tests covering different parts of the site. A sizeable proportion of these – probably as many as 80 per cent need to show a positive uplift on the foreign site, although it doesn't matter if it is not as high as the one gained on the domestic site.

What's important is that both results move in the same general direction.

To illustrate the principle, the table below shows results from two testing programmes, one for a domestic e-commerce website and the same tests rolled out onto an international site.

In the scenario above, you can say with some certainty that the optimization of the international site is 'tightly coupled' to the current optimization of the domestic site.

However, it is still worth doing research and analysis on the international website – even when there is tight coupling – as there is always an opportunity to identify and test hypotheses that could surpass the results

Table 13.2 Example of a tightly coupled optimization process, indicated by split test results moving in a similar direction

	Domestic site – RPV uplift	International site – RPV uplift
Test 1	5.2%	3.1%
Test 2	3.6%	4.1%
Test 3	3.0%	2.2%
Test 4	Inconclusive	Inconclusive
Test 5	8.9%	6.7%
Test 6	−2.3%	−4.5%
Test 7	−9.7%	−11.8%

Table 13.3 Results from a loosely coupled optimization process

	Domestic site – RPV uplift	International site – RPV uplift
Test 1	5.2%	Inconclusive
Test 2	3.6%	–9.8%
Test 3	3.0%	4.2%
Test 4	Inconclusive	8.1%
Test 5	8.9%	–5.5%
Test 6	–2.3%	2.3%
Test 7	–9.7%	3.4%

generated from the domestic site optimization. It is possible that user needs and context are different, and they are potentially affected by different influences given the cultural differences.

Table 13.3 shows the results from a loosely coupled optimization process, where the tests rolled out to the international site didn't replicate the ones run on the domestic site.

In this scenario, the results of the same split tests run on the two sites are not going in the same direction. This is a strong indication that you will need to optimize the two sites separately. The research and analysis of the international website will be the major source of hypothesis generation and testing.

Loosely coupled optimization is likely to occur in sites which operate in countries which have widely different cultures, such as the UK and China.

Facilitating remote moderated usability testing sessions

With the support and assistance of your foreign collaborator, a lot of the research and insight generation can be completed by you. However, one aspect of the research that can only be performed by your foreign collaborator is Remote Moderated Usability Testing (RMUT). If your collaborator is not an experienced researcher, you will need to train them to a high enough standard so that they can conduct the research and gain the insights that you need from this vital research.

Training could be a combination of formal instruction and on-the-job such as:

1 First do some RMUT with your foreign collaborator as the website visitor on your domestic site – start the process with him or her completing the recruitment screener, you getting in touch and completing an entire usability session

2 Let your collaborator shadow you doing RMUT in your language, including how to set up the screen sharing

3 Practise with your collaborator being the facilitator and you the usability participant. Do several sessions together, practise situations where you are both very quiet, clearly not engaged with the task, as well as being a very chatty tester who wants to share their life story

4 Ask your collaborator to facilitate a session while you watch and provide feedback – make sure your collaborator is not leading the participant

We have found in our own testing that some cultures are naturally less willing to make unfavourable comments about your website and their experience of it.

Your collaborator will need to be clear that a usability tester is helping when they are voicing their thoughts and telling him or her about their experience – whether it is positive or negative they want to hear about it. Alternatively, some testers may want to complete the whole usability session in silence, before they share their thoughts about the experience of using the site. Your collaborator will need to regularly prompt testers to share their thoughts if they go quiet.

Changes that will need to be made

Changes to prioritization and test plan

Having the majority of your research, especially the qualitative and voice-of-customer data, translated into English, allows you to prioritize the insights you have and then create an Optimization Plan as you would do for your domestic site.

Changes to creative work and testing

If your split test variation involves extensive copy changes, then use a professional copywriter to develop the copy. This copy should be delivered to the translator free of any English idioms (such as 'popping out' or 'help is at hand') and culturally specific references (eg NHS). This is especially important if you are translating into multiple languages, because it saves the same queries coming in from several translators. Since there's likely to be a small number of words that need to be translated, use your collaborator to do this. S/he will have developed a better understanding of visitors' needs than any third-party agency.

Within the Creative Work and Testing phase there are two opportunities where feedback is sought. Your collaborator will need to gather feedback on the proposed wireframe and web page in the same way as explained in Chapter 7. It is important that feedback gathered in the foreign language is translated so that you are clear what aspects of the proposed split test is being improved and why.

Investing in exhaustive research, using a structured process, with the help of a skilful native language collaborator can help you achieve powerful insights into your international visitors and a healthy uplift in revenue.

Summary

If you run online operations in more than one country, you can use the same principles to optimize them, with some small adaptations for local differences.

Research and analysis is critical because of cultural differences. This is far more than changes to language and payment options. It's about understanding how the needs, thought processes and motivations of your international visitors differ from your domestic ones.

This insight, and the way you choose to optimize your website in a culturally sensitive fashion, can be a source of competitive advantage against the transnational giants, who tend to take the approach of using the same site design, navigation and user experience in every country.

Before deciding to optimize one of your foreign sites, work out whether it is worth it financially. Look at your key metrics for both domestic and international site (or sites), as well as industry data and competitor activity, and your potential costs, before making the decision.

Recruit a native language speaker who can collaborate with you, although accept you may need to train them in some aspects of optimization. Ask your collaborator to verify the quality of any translations.

When you have run some tests on your foreign site, check back and see whether the positive wins on the home site also do well abroad. If they do you could have a tightly coupled optimization process which will save you time and money by just developing one split test for the home site and translating it. If this is not the case then your optimization is loosely coupled which means you will need to have separate optimization programmes for your international and domestic sites.

Notes

1 Marcus, A and Gould, E W (2000) Crosscurrents: Cultural dimensions and global web user interface design, *Interactions*, 7(4), July/August 2000, pp 32–46.

2 Bishop, C (2012) Seven tips for global e-commerce, available from: https://econsultancy.com/blog/9387-7-tips-for-global-ecommerce (accessed: 1 July 2016).

3 Acclaro (2011) Localization gone bad: Marketing missteps, available from: http://www.acclaro.com/blog/localization-gone-bad-marketing-missteps/ (accessed: 1 July 2016).

Launching a new website 14

'We need a better website' is often where it starts.

Switching to a new website, or migrating to a new e-commerce platform, is likely to be one of the biggest capital expenses any 21st century online business could make. Typically, it's a huge investment of time, management resource and money.

It's exciting and naturally comes with high expectations that the effort and expense will be worth it, with improved efficiencies and sales.

All too often though, the reality is somewhat different. Things do go wrong and there are endless ways for the changes to lead to reduced revenue and poorer customer experience.

So what problems are typically encountered? How do you prevent them happening and get the website you're hoping for? And if, despite your best efforts, the website fails to give you higher sales when you launch, what can you do to put it right?

Do you need a new website?

Before you start on a major re-platform or redesign, the first question is whether a new website is required in the first place. Have you fully considered the other option of keeping the current site and investing the resources you might have spent on a new website on optimizing your existing site? It's less exciting but it's far less risky and could actually make you a lot more money.

A brand new website that replaces your existing one with another, that often bears little resemblance to the old website's look and feel, navigation and/or functionality is called a 'Radical Redesign'.

The opposite is 'Evolutionary Site Redesign', which comes about naturally as part of a CRO process. Evolutionary site design gives you continual improvements and increasing online sales in a controlled way.

Figure 14.1   Evolutionary Site Redesign

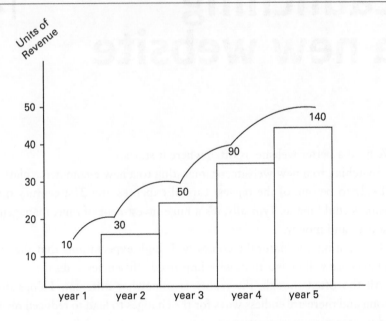

Figure 14.2   Radical Redesign

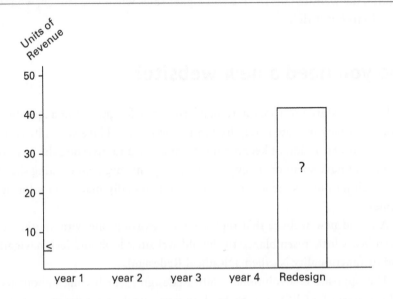

By contrast, radical redesign is typically undertaken every five years, costing large amounts of money and time. The hope is that it will achieve a substantial increase in sales immediately, although this is by no means guaranteed. The figures below illustrate why you make just as much money, if not more, with evolutionary changes, without any of the risks and uncertainties of a brand new, expensive design.

In Evolutionary Site Redesign (ESR) gains are made each year. Any improvements made in Year 1 carry on over the following four years, so revenue growth is cumulative and exponential. To achieve ESR requires a systematic programme of continuous learning, testing and optimization. Since you are verifying each incremental improvement, the extra sales are predictable before they go live on the website.

Radical redesigns are risky. Often there has not been a process of learning and discovery so revenue uplifts are not as predictable. Secondly there is often no clear line of sight between changes to the website and the result they may generate. Once the decision has been taken to invest in a radical redesign there remains a significant question mark as to whether this investment will be repaid.

While we recommend the evolutionary approach there may be times when the radical redesign will be justified:

- The website's underlying technology is severely outdated, eg the website is not responsive or it has been patched so frequently that simple website updates become slow and costly to implement
- The third-party providing website development services on their proprietary platform is slow and expensive and you need to re-platform and start a new relationship with a different supplier
- The design of the website is amateurish and has a negative impact on the standing of the brand
- Results from your optimization efforts show diminishing returns and you have hit your local maxima (first mentioned in Chapter 9)

However, almost certainly for you an evolutionary site redesign would not only be possible but desirable. This is the current practice of most of today's internet giants. The likes of Facebook, Google, Amazon and Ebay continually evolve their current design and functionality.

That's because a radical redesign carries a huge risk. The large financial investment may not be repaid with increased sales.

Or worse. It's quite possible that your new e-commerce site could harm sales, as Marks and Spencer found out to their cost. In 2014, after having invested reportedly over £150m in a new website, on launch, M&S's website immediately suffered a 8 per cent loss in sales.[1] It took the company many months and much work to understand why the website was failing to perform and then to fix the issues to get sales back to their previous level.

When you make large-scale changes to a website's design, navigation and functionality there are often hidden consequences. While some of the changes will increase sales, others will depress them, as Figure 14.3 shows.

If your overall revenue drops, then thorough analysis or testing will be required to discover where the positive improvements and negative impacts are. If the positives outweigh the negatives so that net revenue goes up, these negative pockets are not immediately obvious. They remain unnoticed so they are not investigated, although they represent significant lost opportunity.

Adopting an evolutionary approach to site design offers a number of advantages over radical redesigns as it allows you to:

1 Still get the new 'look and feel' and lift conversion at the same time

2 Get real-time feedback on whether a change is delivering the desired impact or not. If not, you can easily retrace your steps

3 Focus on key business metrics rather than a design which may look aesthetically pleasing but does not perform or offer a good user experience

4 Avoid the financial risks and loss of competitiveness associated with the radical redesign approach

5 Mitigate the risks that your existing customers will be confused by the new radical design and start spending less

6 Work at a faster pace and is a more effective form of optimization than a radical redesign.

7 Offer a website to your customers and visitors that is continually evolving rather than waiting for the typical three to five year gaps between radical redesigns.

However, you may not be in a position to adopt an evolutionary approach to site design, either because of the four reasons listed earlier, or for political reasons management has simply proclaimed 'We need a better website'. It may also be that the business is used to managing projects in the waterfall approach of radical redesign, rather than the modern agile approach.

But what is the impact of the e-commerce website project that goes badly off the rails? To answer this question we commissioned our own research, surveying those with extensive experience of working on these types of projects. The study revealed more than half (55 per cent) of respondents experienced problems working on 'new website and/or functionality' project.

What is clear from our investigation and the M&S example is that launching a new e-commerce website often generates significant problems for the business. The investigation showed that the most common problems when launching a new e-commerce website were:

- loss of sales / revenue
- disgruntled visitors
- management time wasted

These were not isolated incidents, but experienced by over 70 per cent of our respondents.

It is possible to avoid or mitigate these pitfalls by careful management of a radical redesign project. What follows is a step-by-step guide to protect your conversion rates when you create a new e-commerce website and avoid a conversion rate disaster when it's launched.

Five stages of a new website

Our research revealed that the development of an e-commerce website comprises five key stages. Whether you are right at the start and have just got the business case signed off, or whether you are about to go live, there are clear, concrete actions you can take to improve your chances of success after launch.

---

1 Strategy stage: development of a business case
2 Early stage: production of functional specification and identification of suppliers
3 Middle stage: design and development has started
4 Final stage: the run up to launch
5 Live stage: the website has launched

Each stage is different, with a range of beliefs and pitfalls. At any one of these stages decisions will be taken that could seriously harm sales when the new site is launched.

Conversely, there are concrete actions you can take at each stage, to protect your existing conversion rate and make sure the new site performs as well as or better than the current one. And if you have just launched a new site and the worst has happened, there are methods to revive your sales quickly and effectively.

Strategy stage

What happens at the strategy stage?

Typically at the Strategy stage there is an awareness that the website is becoming out of date whilst newer website platforms offer exciting features. Competitors' websites are pored over and sometimes copied wholesale (of course, with no knowledge of exactly how well their website is performing).

A financial case may be developed to weigh up the cost of updating and optimizing your current website versus commissioning a new one – especially if updates are currently slow and costly to make and/or there are no other companies that could take over the maintenance of the website.

Right now, though, this analysis is unlikely to be well-documented and the process of deciding whether to replace the current website has just begun.

Beliefs at the strategy stage

Whilst the decision to replace your current website requires a good deal of thought it is expected that your new website will convert visitors into customers at a much higher rate – why else would this much money be spent?

Expectations are that the new website build, if it happens, will be on time, within budget and deliver substantial ROI.

Pitfalls at the strategy stage

Most of the pitfalls at this stage are around the quality of information available and the assumptions that are being made.

It is common at this stage for there to be little investigation into the cheaper (but less exciting) solution of optimizing the current website. This could be a cost-effective way of replacing the current site. In reality, though, once the decision has been made to commission a new website then any expenditure on the current one often is perceived as 'dead money'.

There is a good deal of excitement around the project and much anticipation of the greener grass on the other side that the new website will offer.

Finally, despite all the nightmare stories that surround new website projects going horribly wrong, there is an overwhelming belief that these disasters only happen to others.

Conversion rate protection at the strategy stage

This early stage may be your best opportunity to gain a high-performing 'new' website at a fraction of the cost of re-platforming or redesigning, so optimization should be given serious consideration.

What factors should influence your decision? It's all down to how much money is being left on the table versus how much could be gained by launching a new website.

What you know is the cost of the new website and by extrapolating previous years' revenue from your current you could forecast likely sales. What you don't know and is hard to predict is the increase you may gain from optimizing the current website. What you can do is conduct a review of the website's weaknesses.

As a recap, here are some of the tools and techniques used to do this kind of evaluation:

- **A conversion funnel** to reliably show where visitors are dropping off
- **Heatmaps** to understand exactly what your visitors click on and what they don't click on
- **Usability testing** with testers recruited directly from the website to understand their experience of the current website in the most revealing way
- **Asking your website visitors and customers** why they abandon / don't buy more from your website (either personally, or with a survey)
- **Asking customers** why they choose to buy from you and not from your competitors?
- **Compiling a list** of how you can strengthen your value proposition to your visitors and customers
- **Benchmarking** your website against your competitors in terms of the strength and weaknesses of your value proposition versus theirs

For more detail on how to research your website and identify conversion killers re-read Chapters 4, 5 and 6.

Having completed this evaluation you will be far more informed about how the current website can be optimized, without the need to invest in a new website. You can then present a detailed analysis as to the costs associated with the new website side-by-side with the untapped opportunities still on the current site.

Early stage protection measures

What happens at the early stage?

This is the stage when the business case has been made for a new e-commerce website/platform and the investment has been agreed in principle. The functional specification is being written, web development partners being appointed and project plans are being finalized.

Although it may seem unthinkable at this point that sales might be lower than at present, it could happen. Here's how you can protect the conversion rate of your website at the early stage.

Beliefs at the early stage

It is tacitly expected that the new website will generate positive ROI and convert at a higher rate than the current one.

It is anticipated that the website will be delivered on time – as there are months to go before the specified delivery date.

Changes to the functional specification can easily be made. At this stage, it's just a document with little set in stone.

Pitfalls at the early stage

These are some of the practices and assumptions we have seen first-hand, that can cause problems later on:

Businesses are overly-influenced by competitors' websites that they believe give their competitors an advantage. However, this can be misleading. The way to stay ahead is to focus on your customers' needs, not what others are doing.

The dunctional specification may be based on industry 'best practice'. (There are many guides and resources offering this kind of advice.) However, these 'one-size-fits-all' techniques may not be right for your website. Website visitors are unique to the business and high-converting websites are designed with their needs at the forefront.

Sometimes a functional specification is based on what the business 'believes' about its website visitors and what they want, rather than being based on rigorous research. So often these hunches and opinions turn out to be simply wrong – or at best do okay, but not as well as a spec based on knowledge of what your real visitors are looking for.

Conversion rate protection at the early stage

The key question to focus on at this stage is 'How can I be sure that the functional specification for the new website is based on the needs of my website users?'

In answering this central question, using similar tools and approaches deployed in the Strategy stage, they will help you clearly state what needs to be fixed on your next website.

You can use all of this evidence to create a Specification Review, which will minimize the risk that the website you are about to commission will fail to deliver. This is because you are cross-checking the functional specification with what you now know about your website customers and visitors.

Middle stage protection measures

What happens at the middle stage?

The Board has signed off the business case and the project is well underway. The functional specification has been written and approved and now design and development have started.

Wireframes have been developed and may already be signed off, together with the look and feel of the template pages and the user flow through the checkout.

Beliefs at the middle stage

This exciting new e-commerce project is well underway, and is set to deliver a new website jam-packed with features and hooks that it is hoped the visitors are going to love.

There is excitement to see how different the new website will be to your current one, and the design is much crisper and more modern – all the ideas the business has had are now crystallized into one perfectly designed website.

The new website will be launched in time for your peak season and you are sure to capitalize on its extra pulling power, turning visitors into customers at a far higher rate.

Pitfalls at the middle stage

Our research shows that these are some of the common issues at this stage:

- Designers and developers are now running the show and, with a strict deadline, many decisions are being taken without much regard to the users of this new website. Making a website look good is not the same as building one that converts well.

- Insufficient thought is being given to the taxonomy of the product categories and sub-categories. The assumption is that this hierarchy is easy to change.

- Copy for products, categories and general static copy is being left until last – just words to fill up the space rather than integral to the customer journey.

The project is now clearly in the delivery phase. The time to make large-scale changes has passed, so anything that was not properly thought through in the early stages can't be put right. Any attempt to do so will affect the launch date.

Conversion rate protection in the middle stage

At this point the central question is 'How can I be sure that this website is going to deliver, without holding up the go-live date?'

In answering this central question, you should consider performing the following quick and easy checks as a Mid-Launch Audit:

- Get the wireframes and mocked-up pages reviewed by actual users of your website. This is quick and inexpensive but will give invaluable feedback. True, you may get one or two red warning lights – but if they are going to seriously affect conversion rate when the site goes live, it's much easier and cheaper to know now.

- Make sure that the copy is professionally written, with the website visitor in mind (not search engine spiders).

- Review the wording around the value proposition of the new website. While the proposition itself should remain constant, there may be a more compelling way of expressing it. Test the new messaging with your customers if you're not sure.

- Analyse the sales performance of categories and sub-categories to ensure that they are in the correct position within the new navigation.

- Perform a look-to-book ratio analysis to see which products require more attention to make them as compelling as others.

Final stage protection measures

What happens in the final stage?

The live date is fast approaching.

It seems light years away since the business case and functional specification were being written. Chances are it's taken longer than everyone expected – for a myriad of reasons that are nobody's fault. (We have yet to hear about a new website that launches on time.)

With the live date quickly approaching, relationships may be fraught, tensions running high and team members can't agree on the priorities.

Beliefs at the final stage

The website is a few days away from being live and although a number of compromises on all sort of things have had to be made it's just a matter of time before you can flick the switch.

Everyone is excited to see how the new website will perform. There is huge expectation that online sales are going to shoot through the roof in the very near future.

Pitfalls at the final stage

The main danger at this point is that compromises the business has been forced to make have affected what the website offers to visitors in terms of frictionless usability and a persuasive experience.

Of course, some of those compromises were necessary, as they could have jeopardized the whole project. But some may actually cause the new website to perform at far lower levels of conversion than before.

We have seen this many times over – the challenge of keeping to a deadline has meant that some companies have inadvertently thrown out the baby with the bathwater. Even worse, they are really not sure which was the baby and which was the bathwater.

Conversion rate protection at the final stage

At this stage, there's no more time left to make changes for launch day. The main focus now should be to ensure funnels are correctly configured so that the customer journey can be analysed. These funnel reports allow you to make revealing comparisons between the current and new website.

Useful metrics for benchmarking include:

- Revenue per Visitor (RPV)
- Bounce Rate for key landing pages (BR)
- Exit Rate (ER)
- Basket Abandonment Rate (AR)
- Add to Basket ratios for your bestsellers (A2B)
- Conversion Rate (CR)

Segment these metrics by new and returning visitors, by your five most popular traffic sources and by device type.

We very much hope your conversion will not drop when the new site goes live. But we've seen it happen many times. If you are unlucky enough that it happens to you, you'll be one step ahead, because you'll know exactly where your customers are dropping out compared with the old site.

Also do some usability testing with your website visitors. You won't be able to use their input to make changes to the new site but it will mean you have a good idea of which elements of the new website are the most important ones to fix as soon as you go live – elements that matter to your website visitors, not you.

Live stage protection measures

If you have jumped straight to this section, it is probably because you have got a conversion disaster on your hands – and you're really not sure what to do.

What happens in the live stage?

If conversion and sales are going up, there is jubilation. But if the numbers are all heading south, it's a real anti-climax. Everyone is disappointed that their months of work has not paid off and morale is low. The finance team may be looking at the money spent and wondering how it was justified for a website that is, seemingly, worse than the one it replaced.

If this has happened, despite all best efforts and smart planning, what can be done?

Sometimes the answer is obvious – the funnel tells you that a lot of visitors are dropping out at checkout stage or there is an issue with page load speed.

At other times it's not clear. The site loads quickly, looks great and performs functionally, but visitors are just not buying like they used to.

Beliefs at the live stage

Plunging sales create an urgent requirement to do something to address the issue – and to do it quickly. Everyone is looking for leadership and a sensible course of action, that will attack the issue at its core – where is the problem and what are we going to do about it. The time for guesswork has passed and everyone is expecting the way forward to be based on data and evidence.

Pitfalls at the live stage

As with any crisis the biggest problem is likely to be the blame game, blind panic and grasping at straws. Every minute needs to be focused on understanding the conversion problem and its root causes.

Your analytic reports will tell you where the problems exist between the new and old site but they won't tell why these problems exist. By using voice-of-customer tools, like surveys and usability testing with real visitors, you can develop valid hypotheses to test to fix the problems.

Conversion rate protection at the live stage

The right approach at this stage is to have a plan – and to stick to it. The infographic below shows a step-by-step guide to rescuing a poorly performing new website, sensibly and systematically.

Just like an effective CRO programme you install tools on your site for research and analysis, as well as split testing tools to test your hypotheses.

But, why put yourself in this situation? Why risk everything, when you can simply optimize the site you've got, make your customers happy and reap the rewards. We've shared with you everything you need to put your own CRO programme in place. Follow what we've told you and it will work. The future is in your hands, and we hope you enjoy the exciting and prosperous journey ahead.

Summary

Our experience is that in the majority of cases you will gain a greater and quicker return on investment by continuously optimizing your e-commerce website, and going for evolutionary redesign rather than the radical redesign

Figure 14.3   Conversion Disaster Recovery Programme

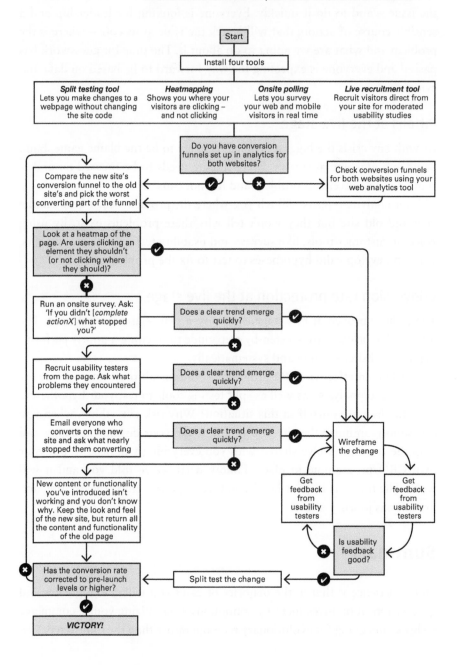

of a brand new website. Of course there are times when a radical redesign is unavoidable, but it is always worth investigating whether a redesign will bring higher rewards than an evolutionary approach.

There are five stages to launching a new website, and there are pitfalls at each one. You can mitigate the risks by taking protective actions. These actions split into two main approaches.

At the Strategy, Early and Mid stages, focus is on understanding your website visitors and customers and ensuring that their needs will be delivered by the new website.

Later on, at the Final and Live stages, focus on checking whether there are any negative effects caused by the new website. Research why these pages are causing visitor dropout and then launch split tests to test fixes that will reverse the decline in sales.

A new website always carries risks, so we recommend you instead opt for Conversion Rate Optimization whenever possible as it's a much surer bet. We have given you the tools to run your own CRO programme and wish you every success.

Note

1 Wood, Z (2014) Shareholders attack Marks & Spencer as website revamp loses customers, available from: http://www.theguardian.com/business/2014/jul/08/marks-and-spencer-shareholders-attack-website-online-sales-fall (accessed: 1 July 2016).

FURTHER READING

If you would like to explore the topics we covered in this book in more detail, below is a list of useful books that we recommend.

Ash, T, Page, R and Ginty, M (2012) *Landing Page Optimization: the definitive guide to testing and tuning for conversions*, J Wiley & Sons, Indianapolis

Burby, J and Atchison, S (2007) *ActionabLE WEB ANAlytics: Using data to make smart business decisions*, J Wiley & Sons, Indianapolis

Caldwell, L (2012) *The Psychology of Price: How to use price to increase demand, profit and customer satisfaction*, Crimson Publishing, Richmond

Cialdini, RB (2007) *Influence: The Psychology of Persuasion*, HarperCollins, New York

Clifton, B (2012) *Advanced Web Wetrics with Google Analytics*, 3rd edn, J Wiley & Sons, Indianapolis

Colborne, G (2010) *Simple and Wsable Web, Wobile, and Wnteraction Wesign*, New Riders Publishing

Davenport, TH and Harris, JG (2007) *Competing on Wnalytics: The new science of winning*, Harvard Business School Press, Boston

Davenport, TH, Harris, JG and Morison, R (2009) *Analytics at Work: Smarter decisions, better results*, Harvard Business Review Press, Boston

Dooley, R (2011) *Brainfluence: 100 ways to persuade and convince consumers with neuromarketing*, J Wiley & Sons

Duarte, DL and Snyder, NT (2006) *Mastering Wirtual Teams: Strategies, tools and techniques that succeed* , 3rd edn, John Wiley & Sons, San Francisco

Eisenberg, B and Eisenberg, J (2006) *Call to Action: Secret formulas to improve online results*, Thomas Nelson

Eisenberg, B, Eisenberg, J and Davis, LT (2006) *Waiting for Your cat to Bark? Persuading customers when they ignore marketing*, Thomas Nelson Publishers, Nashville

Few, S (2004) *Show Me the Numbers: Designing tables and graphs to enlighten*, ed Nan Wishner, Analytics Press, Oakland

Goward, C (2013) *You Should Test That: Conversion optimization for more leads, sales and revenue or the art and science of optimized marketing*, J Wiley & Sons, Hoboken

Hunt, B (2011) *Convert!: Designing web sites to increase traffic and conversion*, J Wiley & Sons, Indianapolis

Jackson, S (2009) *Cult of Analytics: Driving online marketing strategies using web analytics*, Routledge

Jarrett, C and Gaffney, G (2009) *Forms that Work: Designing web forms for usability*, Morgan Kaufmann Publishers

Kahneman, D (2012) *Thinking, Fast and Slow*, Penguin

Kaushik, A (2009) *Web Analytics 2.0: The art of online accountability and science of customer centricity*, J Wiley & Sons, Indianapolis

Kostner, J (1996) *Virtual Leadership: Secrets from the round table for the multi-site manager*, Grand Central Publishing

Krug, S (2009) *Rocket Surgery Made Easy: The do-it-yourself guide to finding and fixing usability problems*, New Riders Publishing, Berkeley

Krug, S (2013) *Don't Make Me Think: A Common sense approach to web usability*, 3rd edn, New Riders Publishing

Laja, P (2013) *How to Build Websites that Sell: The scientific approach to websites*, Hyperink: Blog to Book

Loveday, L and Niehaus, S (2007) *Web Design for ROI: Turning browsers into buyers and prospects into leads*, New Riders Publishing, Berkeley

Massey, B (2012) *Your Customer Creation Equation: Unexpected website formulas of the conversion scientist TM*, CMI Books, Division of Z Squared Media

Mulder, S and Yaar, Z (2006) *The User is Always Right: A practical guide to creating and using personas for the web*, New Riders Publishing

Nahai, N (2012) *Webs of Influence: The psychology of online persuasion*, Pearson Education

Nielsen, J and Loranger, H (2006) *Prioritizing web usability*, New Riders Publishing

Page, R (2012) *Website Optimization: An hour a day*, J Wiley & Sons, Hoboken

Peterson, ET (2004) *Web Analytics Demystified: A marketer's guide to understanding how your web site affects your business*, Celilo Group Media

Peterson, ET (2005) *Web Site Measurement Hacks: Tips and tools to help optimize your online business*, O'Reilly

Pfeffer, J and Sutton, R (2013) *The Knowing-Doing Gap: How smart companies turn knowledge into action*, Harvard Business School Press

Quarto-von Tivadar, J, & Eisenberg, B (2008), *Always Be Testing: The complete guide to Google website optimizer*, J Wiley & Sons

Rosenfeld, L (2011) *Search Analytics for Your Site: Conversations with your customers*, Rosenfeld Media

Spencer, D (2009) *Card Sorting: Designing usable categories*, Rosenfeld Medi

Sterne, J (2002) *Web Metrics: Proven methods for measuring website success*, J Wiley & Sons

Tonkin, S, Whitmore, C and Cutroni, J (2011) *Performance Marketing with Google Analytics: Strategies and techniques for maximizing online ROI*, J Wiley & Sons, New York

Tulathimutte, T and Bolt, N (2014) *Remote Research*, Rosenfeld Media

Underhill, P (2004) *Why We Buy: The science of shopping*, Simon & Schuster, New York

Weinschenk, SM (2008) *Neuro Web Design: What makes them click? (voices that matter series)*, New Riders Publishing, Berkeley

Wroblewski, L (2011) *Mobile First*, A Book Apart, New York

ADDITIONAL ACKNOWLEDGEMENTS

The authors and publisher gratefully acknowledge the following companies for allowing their content to be referenced within this book.

Qubit

Qubit is the pioneer in delivering data-first customer experiences. By bringing together analytics, data and experience management, Qubit's digital experience hub offers a blank canvas for businesses to deliver their big ideas. Their infrastructure is built from the ground up to deliver an integrated workflow so that teams can work more fluidly together and intelligent customer experiences can be delivered across every brand touchpoint.

LiftSuggest

The LiftSuggest team at Tatvic – www.tatvic.com – generously provided their services for the price A/B testing tool.

INDEX